REALTOR®
FOR LIFE

Duane Duggan

Visit Duane Duggan's website at www.boulderpropertynetwork.com.

10 9 8 7 6 5 4 3 2 1

Library of Congress Cataloging-in-Publication Data is available on file.

Print ISBN-13 978-1518858185, ISBN-10 151885818X

Printed in the United States of America

PREFACE

What's it mean to be a REALTOR® for Life?

First of all, an agent needs to become a REALTOR®! Not all real estate agents are REALTORS®. The term REALTOR® is the exclusive designation of members of the National Association of REALTORS® and it's local boards. REALTOR® is listed in the US patent office as a registered trademark. Licensing is just the first step in an agent's career. Once an agent makes the commitment to being a REALTOR®, they subscribe to the REALTORS® Code of Ethics, which was first adopted in 1913. Knowing and following the Code of Ethics sets the REALTOR® member apart from other real estate professionals. Since 1913, The Code of Ethics has evolved and changes are usually made each year to keep up with new issues in the real estate industry. REALTORS are required to take an ethics refresher course every four years to keep abreast of the changes.

The Code of Ethics is known as the "golden thread" of the industry, dedicated to raising the standards of professionalism and service in real estate. The Code provides a guide for how REALTORS® interact with each other, and work toward furthering clients' interests. Since 2013, The Code consists of 17 Articles, 71 Standards of Practice, and 131 explanatory cases. An individual REALTOR® member's local Board of REALTORS® is responsible for enforcing the code.

REALTOR® for Life from my point of view

The majority of REALTORS® have had other careers before going "into real estate". For some reason, my first year of college, I declared my major to be in Business with an emphasis in Real Estate. I became a REALTOR® and started selling real estate as my first position out in the work world. As of 2015, I have been a REALTOR® for 37 years, truly a REALTOR® for my entire business life.

REALTOR ® for Life from the client's point of view

One of the most rewarding parts of my career is that many of my clients have chosen me to be their REALTOR® for Life. Often, I have met someone and helped them buy their first home. I have helped some clients buy 3 or 4 personal residences in their life. In some cases I am even preparing to work with the 3rd generation of clients in a family! In addition to buying homes, I have also helped them build real estate portfolios. I have helped them save for college or retirement through real estate. I have helped them buy real estate within their retirement account and do 1031 Exchanges to grow their portfolio. I've helped find college condos for their kids.   Because I have met and know thousands of REALTORS® personally I help them find a REALTOR® wherever they know anyone buying or selling across the country and now the globe. Toward the end of their life, I help with consolidating real estate investments, down sizing, and ultimately working with their estate planning attorney. More than once I have been named in a will to be the REALTOR® to sell the house.

As REALTORS®, we always need to keep in mind we are not attorneys, tax experts, mortgage loan officers, security dealers or financial planners. It is important to know about all the various ideas discussed in this book, but also very important to have a team of experts that you can rely upon to help your clients with their decisions relative to the areas that we are not licensed to perform.

The main intent of this book is to help you be the trusted advisor for your clients on all matters real estate, and in return they will call you their "REALTOR® for Life". I want to provide you with a resource that you can read all the way through and then keep ready as a reference. My hope is that you will get an idea from this book that will enhance your or your client's life.

TESTIMONIALS

"This book is the next best thing to a step-by-step manual on how to stay relevant with past and future clients. If you ever wondered how to reach out with intelligent, warm touches, read this book! In fact, we have used it as a basis for monthly mailing to our clients."

Tupper Briggs
Re/Max Alliance Evergreen

"I have bought and sold over a dozen homes for my personal residences. Purchased, renovated and sold another dozen fix & flips successfully and bought & sold our currently owned multi-family properties. Most of these transactions involved working with Duane (some were in other cities) and he has always been knowledgeable, professional and courteous making an oft times difficult situation enjoyable. The information in this book is comprehensive, accurate, detailed and will be a great source of knowledge whether you are a REALTOR® for life or a budding real estate investor."

Scott Woodard, President
Fit Properties, Boulder CO

"I really admire his career long dedication to perfecting his craft. It really shows he has his client's best interest at heart! Congrats Duane!"

Rick Miller
Account Manager
Land Title Guarantee Company, Boulder CO

"As the manager at REMAX of Boulder, I supervise over 100 REALTORS®. I see this book as a basis of knowledge for any REALTOR® trying to be their client's Realtor® for life."

DB Wilson
Managing Broker
REMAX of Boulder, Boulder CO

"This book is incredible! It is a step-by-step guide full of valuable information for new or experienced REALTORS® . Duane is a master at his craft and it shows in his book!"

Eric Thompson
President
Windermere Services Colorado

"In our "on-demand" society, NO ONE wants to wait 38 years to gain valuable experience, and now you don't have to wait. REALTOR® for Life is your playbook for success. Duane Duggan's book provides wisdom to everyone; from new real estate agents to seasoned veterans. I am proud to call Duane a client, my mentor, and a friend."

Kyle Malnati
REALTOR® *Magazine* National "30 Under 30" Winner
Madison & Company Properties

"Duane Duggan is the 'real deal.' He 'walks the talk' of real estate and has systematized his business so he can enjoy the quality of life he envisioned for himself and his family all those years ago when he started. Whenever I talk to young people who are considering a career in real estate, I point to Duane Duggan as the epitome of how to succeed. I wish I'd had this book 23 years ago when I started my second career as a Realtor."

Lisa Wade
RE/MAX of BOULDER
Broker Associate
BARA President 2014/2015
BARA Realtor of the Year 2013

"I just finished Duane's new book and wanted to let you know how much I enjoyed reading it. The section on investments for college funds and college-aged family members was perfect for my market. I'm using your ideas to send out a marketing piece to my clients. I find myself going back to the book again and again to pull out jewels to use in my business and marketing. I just wish you wrote the book 22 years ago when I first entered the real estate business."

Scott Miller
Realtor
Boulder, CO

REALTOR FOR LIFE

CONTENTS

 Financing & Finances

 Real Estate Investing

 The Real Estate Market

INTRODUCTION i

REALTOR® for Life

When you get out of license school, your state government has branded you as an "Expert" in the field of real estate. However, having your license is just the first step in educating yourself to becoming a successful REALTOR®.

Definition of an "Expert"

A home auto enthusiast was working on his engine and couldn't get it to work, so he called in an expert. The expert took a hammer, hit it in the right spot, and with just the right amount of intensity and the engine suddenly worked. The expert said that will be $100. The person said, that's ridiculous, it just took you one second. Yes, the expert said, but it's all in knowing where and how hard to hit it.

If you go to a hardware store and ask for a hammer, the clerk immediately asks you what kind. Carpenter, ball peen, finishing, sledge etc. Then you need to pick a size. Having just the right tool makes a huge difference in the ease of the job at hand and of course the end result.

The intent of this book is to give you the tools that you need to succeed in your real estate business and to help your clients achieve their real estate goals. In many cases, an idea presented may be just the "hammer." However, I hope that I give you enough drive to seek other types of "hammers," that may help you expand on a particular topic. For example, in my chapter on real estate exchanges (the hammer), there are several different types (different hammers) of exchanges that can be done. So not only do I hope to be able to help you pick the right size and style of hammer, but also give you the education so you'll know how "Hard to hit," and where to investigate further if necessary.

Transactional Approach vs. the REALTOR® for Life Approach

The approach most agents use in their business is the transactional approach. That involves just selling a home as a personal residence to the clients and then moving on to the next one. Over the years, I have learned to become involved with my client's lives, in order to help them with different real estate transactions as they go through life. A REALTOR® typically first meets clients to help them with their personal residence. As a REALTOR® gets to know the client, they might discover that they want to buy an investment property as an avenue for saving for a child's college education. The client may want to buy a condo for their college student to live in while they attend college. Or maybe the client would invest in real estate using their IRA funds if their REALTOR® informs them of that possibility. The list of options for how a REALTOR® might help a client with real estate needs, beyond their personal residence, is quite extensive. **The typical client doesn't know all the different ways their REALTOR® can help, so it's up to the REALTOR® to educate them on all the opportunities that are available.** Internet lead generation has made the transactional approach even more typical. Get the lead, close it, and move on to the next one. It is our challenge to make sure our clients are well informed about all that is available to them.

MORTGAGE ACCELERATION   **1**

The first closing with your clients

As mentioned before, the first closing a REALTOR® has with a client is usually for the client's personal residence. At the closing table it is always a bit of a joke when the happy home buyers are asked to sign the loan disclosures showing how much interest they will pay over the life of their 30 year loan. Often times they say things like "oh, I'll be dead by then anyway", or " wow, I had no idea!". As your client's "REALTOR® for Life", this is your first opportunity to help your clients create a system to build equity and real estate wealth by teaching them about Mortgage Acceleration.

Mortgage Acceleration

The ideas on mortgage acceleration have changed many times over the years. The depression era generation celebrated mortgage-burning parties when the final payment was made. The next generation came along, kept mortgage balances high for tax deductibility, and in theory, "invested" the cash for a better return. Then came the next generation, with home values skyrocketing, they used their homes as cash machines, pulling cash out for consumer items and lengthening the term of their loan, and in theory, never paying off their mortgage. This resulted with many losing their home to foreclosure. So which generation is smartest? The answer is not so simple. It takes quite a bit of study to figure it out.

What if you or your clients had no mortgage on your property? Would their life be any different? Could you invest that cash flow that would have gone into mortgage payments into something else?

There are many ways to accelerate the payoff of a mortgage and there are just as many considerations as to whether or not to pay one off early at all. But first, let's take a look at how mortgage amortization works.

On a $100,000 Loan at 6% you could pay the loan off according to the following schedule:

Term	Monthly Payment
30 yrs.	$599.55
20 yrs.	$716.43
15 yrs.	$843.86
10 yrs.	$1110.21
5 yrs.	$1933.28
3 yrs.	$3042.19

How much interest do you pay on a $100,000 loan over 30 years?

Term	# Payments	Monthly Payment	Total Paid	Amount paid in Interest
30 yrs.	360	$599.55	$215,838.00	$115,838.00
20 yrs.	240	$716.43	$171,943.20	$71,943.20
15 yrs.	180	$843.86	$151,894.80	$51,894.80
10 yrs.	120	$1110.21	$133,225.20	$33,225.20
5 yrs.	60	$1933.28	$115,996.80	$15,996.80
3 yrs.	36	$3042.19	$109,518.84	$9,518.84

What if I pay $100 more a month on a $100,000 30-year loan at 6%? Pay $699.55 a month instead of $599.55. This shortens the loan to 252 payments instead of 360 or **9 years less**! That would mean 108 payments of $599.55 a month that you didn't need to make, saving $64,751.

Now all that sounds wonderful, but there are two factors not taken into consideration: deductibility of interest on a tax return and the time value of money.

Tax savings factor

In the first year of a $100,000, 30-year mortgage at 6% you pay $5967 in interest and $1228 in principal. The interest is deductible on your tax return. So if you are in the 30% tax bracket times the amount of interest paid ($5967) the amount of tax savings for that year would be $1790.

Now, the clincher to this factor is actually taking the amount of tax savings and investing that amount! Which of course, most people don't do!

Time Value of Money factor

Consider that instead of paying more on your mortgage in advance, you take that money and invest it in a safe place at a 6% rate. Let's take the example of choosing to pay down an extra $100 a month on the mortgage or investing that same $100 a month in something that earned 6%.

If you invested $100/month for 30 years it would generate a cash account of $100,451.50. Again, the main factor is that the typical person doesn't have the discipline to do this. If inflation were to stay at 4% a year for the next 30 years, the value of a dollar 30 years from now will be $.30. So the argument is that you are paying off a dollar in the future with only $.30.

What isn't taken into account is what if you had no mortgage payment after 7 years, as an example, and invested what would have been the entire monthly payment?

On a $100,000 loan:
- To pay off in 7 years, at 6% interest, the monthly payment required is $1460.87
- The 30-year amortized payment is $599.55
- $1460.87 - $599.55 = $861.32 that you use to pay off the mortgage instead of investing.
- When the mortgage is paid off in 7 years, invest the $861.32 a month for the next 23 years at 6%.
- At the end of 30 years you have $510,118.02 in the bank instead of $0.
- For a present value (based on 4% inflation for 30 years) it is still $108,075.62 in today's dollars.

Combine the tax savings factor and "Time Value of Money" factor

As each year goes by, the amount of interest goes down and the amount of tax savings decreases. There is no way to know exactly what your tax rate will be each year, but still, you do have tax savings that continues each year. If you are more of a visual person, see page 4 to see what a 30-year amortized loan looks like.

AMORTIZATION SCHEDULE
FOR A 30-YEAR LOAN AT 6%

YEAR	BALANCE	INTEREST	PRINCIPLE
1	$98,772	$5,967	$1,228
2	$97,468	$5,891	$1,304
3	$96,084	$5,810	$1,384
4	$94,615	$5,725	$1,470
5	$93,054	$5,634	$1,560
6	$91,398	$5,538	$1,656
7	$89,639	$5,436	$1,759
8	$87,772	$5,328	$1,867
9	$85,790	$5,212	$1,982
10	$83,686	$5,090	$2,104
11	$81,451	$4,960	$2,234
12	$79,079	$4,823	$2,372
13	$76,561	$4,676	$2,518
14	$73,887	$4,521	$2,674
15	$71,049	$4,356	$2,839
16	$68,035	$4,181	$3,014
17	$64,836	$3,995	$3,200
18	$61,439	$3,798	$3,397
19	$57,832	$3,588	$3,606
20	$54,004	$3,366	$3,829
21	$49,939	$3,130	$4,065
22	$45,623	$2,879	$4,316
23	$41,041	$2,613	$4,582
24	$36,177	$2,330	$4,864
25	$31,012	$2,030	$5,164
26	$25,529	$1,712	$5,483
27	$19,708	$1,373	$5,821
28	$13,528	$1014	$6,180
29	$6,966	$633	$6531
30	$0	$228	$6966
TOTAL		$115,838	$100,000

Mortgage Acceleration

1. Create your own amortization schedule to pay it off in the desired number of years

On a $100,000 Loan at 6% you could pay the loan off according to the following schedule:

Term	Monthly Payment
30 years	$599.55
20 years	$716.43
15 years	$843.86
10 years	$1,110.21
5 years	$1,933.28
3 years	$3,042.19

2. Bi-weekly mortgage payments program

The way that this program works is that when you make a payment every two weeks, you actually put enough in that it would be equivalent to making one extra payment a year. This program will usually pay off a 30-year mortgage in about 7 years sooner. Some lenders offer a bi-weekly mortgage payment plan. You can call your lender to see if they offer a bi-weekly plan. Some lenders will offer the program for free. If your lender doesn't offer a program, there are 3rd party companies that can set up a program for a reasonable fee.

3. One extra payment a year program

On a bi-weekly program it is about the same as making one extra payment a year. So what about just making that extra payment once a year? You can do that and accomplish about the same thing without having to pay for or set up a bi-weekly program.

4. Mortgage acceleration programs

Mortgage acceleration programs, such as the one utilized by a company called United First Financial, uses the first mortgage that is in place on a home, a home equity line of credit, and what is called money merge account software.

This program utilizes a line of credit like a primary checking account. An important function of this line of credit is what is called an open-end interest calculation. By putting your monthly paycheck in toward paying down the line of credit balance, it keeps the balance that interest is calculated on low. By keeping the balance lower, more of the monthly payment is attributed to principal rather than interest. The program helps you manage your money and tells you when would be the best time to make a lump sum payment toward your mortgage principal. You can check out information on this program at www.unitedfirstfinancial.com.

Summary

Everyone needs to decide for themselves if they want to get their mortgage paid off or keep their balance high. Everyone's situation is a little different, so it is a good idea to consult their individual advisors and generate their own set of goals.

SAVING FOR THE NEXT REAL ESTATE PURCHASE   **2**

This concept seems so simple that you have to wonder why it is even included in this book! However, most of America lives paycheck to paycheck. Many were never taught the concept of saving money and of those who were taught, even fewer actually do it!

Your first time buyer has finally put together enough down payment for their first house and has just spent it at closing. One of your first follow up lunches should be to meet with them to talk about saving for their next real estate investment. They might have bought into the mortgage acceleration techniques and are building equity that can be used to purchase the next real estate investment. In the mean time, they should open up an investment account and start accumulating cash! So how do you show them how they can do that?

Pay Yourself First
First, teach them about the "pay yourself first" concept. The government is already into this. When anyone gets a paycheck, the government gets withholding and gets paid first. Next, a portion of anyone's paycheck should go into an investment account, even if it starts out at $100 a month.

The Latte Factor
Teach them about how to determine what their "latte factor" is. That coffee latte habit could be taking $20 a week. Combine that with eliminating car washes, shirt ironing, meals out, etc., it might be easy to suddenly be saving $500 a month toward the next down payment. It is all about priorities!

Automaticity
It needs to happen automatically, too! In other words, automatic withdrawals from the checking account each month into the investment account is a perfect way to start accumulating that nest egg.

REFINANCE OR NOT? 3

When interest rates drop, one wonders whether or not it makes any sense to refinance. Unfortunately, there are many different "rules of thumb" being thrown out to the public to answer the question, "When is the right time to refinance?"

One of these "rules of thumb" says that if your current mortgage loan is less than two years old, you should not refinance. Generally, this thought comes from the fact that closing costs were just paid and when the refinance occurs there will be another set of closing costs. Another common "rule" used to determine the feasibility of refinancing is that there should be at least a 2% spread between the old interest rate and the new refinance rate. The reasoning behind this rule is that at least a 2% difference in interest rates is usually needed in order to justify the expenses incurred when refinancing.

In reality, refinancing your home mortgage could be done any time there is a significant savings in your monthly mortgage payment (or in your overall debt payments if you are consolidating other loans by refinancing) AND you plan to live in your home long enough to recover the expenses incurred with refinancing.

Let's say that your current home mortgage is at a rate of 7%. A refinanced mortgage rate of 5.5% may currently be available to you. Before proceeding with refinancing your current mortgage you need to answer three questions in order to make a wise decision:

1. What are the total costs involved in refinancing?

2. How long do you foresee owning this home?

3. How many more payments will the loan be extended by?

There will be a variety of costs incurred when refinancing a home mortgage. These include: a title policy to assure the lender that they have an enforceable deed of trust and loan on the property, an appraisal to determine your home's market value, a loan origination fee, loan discount points, possible attorney's fees, and a few other miscellaneous fees.

Most title companies will offer a reduced title policy premium when the title insurance is re-issued for an owner within two years of the original title policy issue. This offer is possible because there is less exposure to the title company over such a short period of time.

Most homeowners, upon purchasing a home, find out that any loan discount points paid are deductible as interest by the buyer in the year that they are paid. What may not be generally known is that discount points paid to refinance a home **are not** fully deductible in the year they are paid. These must be prorated or spread out over the life of the mortgage. For example, if a homeowner paid $3,000 in loan discount points to refinance their home mortgage at a lower rate, they could potentially deduct $100 in interest each year for a 30-year mortgage. This would mean a $28/year tax savings if in the 28% tax bracket or $15/year tax savings if in the 15% tax bracket. The downside is that the homeowner had to pay $3,000 either in cash or by adding this amount to the mortgage. If possible, it is generally recommended that homeowners refinance with a "par value" loan, or in other words, that they refinance at a rate which does not require the payment of any loan discount points. This keeps the out of pocket expenses of refinancing at a minimum even though the interest rate may be slightly higher.

It is necessary to understand two terms in order to determine whether the interest payments on a home mortgage are fully deductible: "Acquisition debt" and "Home Equity debt". Acquisition debt is the amount of money borrowed in order to buy, build, or make capital improvements to a principal or second home. The deductibility limit for acquisition debt is $1,000,000 for the combination of a first and second home. As the principal is paid down on this mortgage, the acquisition debt is reduced.

Home Equity debt has a deductibility limit of $100,000 above the current acquisition costs for both the first and second homes. Money pulled out of a home's equity can be used for any purpose including home improvements, education and medical expenses, business expenses, or restructuring and paying off other debts.

When a homeowner refinances a mortgage the acquisition debt does not increase. For example, if a person originally borrowed $175,000 to purchase their home and the current unpaid balance is now

$150,000, the acquisition debt is now $150,000. By refinancing only the $150,000 balance the interest payments will still be deductible.

Assuming the market value of the home will allow it, the homeowner could borrow up to $250,000 and still have all of the interest payments be deductible. $150,000 of the new loan would still be considered acquisition debt and the additional $100,000 would be considered home equity debt.

An important thing for homeowners to be aware of is that all of the interest payments on a principal or second home mortgage may not be tax deductible even though a mortgage company may be willing to make a certain loan amount. The limit restrictions for "acquisition" and "home equity" debt must be taken into consideration and your tax advisor should be consulted for current tax rules.

Due to the competitive nature of the home mortgage business, some lenders will offer "Low" or "No Closing Costs" loans. These types of loans will typically have a slightly higher interest rate. It is important to find out if the lender is actually not charging any closing costs or if these costs are being added to the refinanced mortgage amount. Adding closing costs to the mortgage can hide potentially high loan fees that increase the overall costs of the mortgage, even though the out of pocket expenses are kept low.

When refinancing, the payment can drop for reasons other than interest rate. One is that if the old loan was amortized, the principal is being paid down a bit each month. When the refinance loan is done, the balance will be lower than the original, unless cash is pulled out or if the original loan was interest only. Second, by refinancing, the loan repayment process starts over at 30 years to go. Therefore, much of the monthly savings is tacked on to the end of the loan. Some people will argue the "time value of money". In other words, those dollars added on the end are worth much less than dollars today, hence the argument, "don't pay your mortgage off early".

In summary:
1. Consider refinancing whenever it creates a significant monthly savings and you can recover the expenses of refinancing during the time you own the home.

2. Consider a "par value" loan to keep closing costs at a minimum and be aware that loan points paid when refinancing are not fully deductible as interest in the first year.

3. Be aware of the "home equity debt" limits, all of the interest payments may or may not be fully deductible.

Hopefully this chapter has brought out some key points for you to consider when deciding whether or not to refinance your home mortgage. Please utilize this information as a general overview of refinancing only, it is not to be considered as specific advice for any one person's situation. Due to the complexities involved in the tax laws and to the many individual differences in homeownership situations, I strongly urge you to consult a tax specialist concerning how refinancing can affect any personal situation. However, you can start by using the following worksheet:

REFINANCE OR NOT FORMULA

Current mortgage payment (monthly):	1. $
New mortgage payment (monthly):	2. $
Subtract line 2 from line 1:	3.
Estimated closing costs (typically 2-3% of the new loan)	4. $
Divide line 4 by line 3. The result is the # of months it will take you to recoup your closing costs:	5.
Number of months do you plan to live in your home:	6.

RESULTS:
If the **number on line 6 is at least 12 months more than the number on line 5**, call your current lender to see what they will do. Comparison shop by calling a couple of other lenders.

EQUITY MANAGEMENT   **4**

The question many people ask is, "Should I pay off my mortgage or borrow against the house and invest the cash?"

My parents grew up in the generation where it was important to get the mortgage paid off, and in fact even have a mortgage burning party. When I was in college, I learned about the deductibility of mortgage interest, keeping the mortgage balance high, and investing cash from mortgage proceeds. Now, with the mortgage issues of the 2000s, many people are of the frame of mind to get their mortgages paid off.

Regardless of your point of view, it is important to learn about equity management in your home. In many cases homeowners will pull cash equity out of their home to spend on consumer items, vacations etc. True equity management involves pulling equity out of your home and INVESTING it in the proper investment vehicles. After all, equity has no rate of return unless you activate it! Invest in "what grows" not in "what shows"! Get that real estate investment instead of that flashy sports car! Equity in real estate grows as a result of the loan being paid down and values increasing. But remember, equity itself, does not have a rate of return! Combine the proper investments with mortgage acceleration techniques and the deductibility of mortgage interest, and you have a powerful wealth-building tool.

Earlier, we talked about getting the mortgage on a home paid off. If extra payments are made, the principal definitely goes down faster. But what if tough times were encountered and you wanted money back? You can't call up the lender and say, "I've been paying extra principal, can I have some of it back?". That is an argument for investing what could have been made in extra principal payments, into something that was accessible if cash needs arise.

Let's take a step back for a second and look at a few concepts which I learned from my financial planner, Karl Frank of A and I Financial Services:

Interest on a home that is usually deductible is simple interest with the loan declining each month. If it is deductible the effective interest rate is less than the face rate. When equity is pulled out and that cash is invested, it is invested in something that earns compound interest. This is the opposite of simple interest. If it is possible to invest in something that earns compound interest in a tax-favored environment, then the potential for growth is incredible! Combine all 3 of those factors and what you have is activated equity! Karl's firm has a plan which they call "OUR plan". OUR stands for **O**ptimized **U**niversal Life Insurance Supplemental **R**etirement Plan.

Advantages With "OUR Plan"
- You get life insurance protection, death benefit.
- Your investment grows tax free within the life insurance policy.
- You can withdraw without tax burden up to the original dollar investment OR Withdraw tax free with a policy loan!

The bottom line is that you will build a nice nest egg using this technique!

You can contact Karl Frank at (303) 690-5070 or karl@assetsandincome.com.

INTEREST ONLY MORTGAGES   **5**

When a market accelerates, interest only mortgages become more commonplace. This is because prices are accelerating faster than salaries and the consumer looks for ways to afford a home. Interest only mortgages got a bit of a bad rap because consumers were missing out on getting the loan paid down.

However, there is definitely a time and place to use the interest only loan as a tool for your clients.

One example I have is when I had a client that had been laid off from his job. This client had some other income but the fully amortized payment was making things pretty tight. By using an interest only mortgage they were able to reduce the payment and stay in their home.

A feature that interest only loans have is that if you prepay any principal, the next month, the interest only payment is based on the remaining principal balance. That means the payment goes down immediately. That is a big difference from a 30 year amortized loan. On a 30 year amortized loan, if you prepay principal, it reduces the term of the loan, but the payment remains the same. With the interest only loan, if you are disciplined enough with making extra principal payments, the monthly loan payment will go down each time you do. I found that as a great feature on investment property because the cash flow would keep improving each time you paid the loan down a little bit.

MORTGAGE OFFSET ACCOUNT   **6**

Instead of doing mortgage acceleration techniques discussed earlier, another alternative is to create what I call a mortgage offset account.

One of the advantages of the Mortgage offset account is that you can get the money back if you need it! If you just pay down the mortgage, you can't call the lender and ask for your prepayments back!

How it might work:
Let's say there is a $200,000 mortgage on a house. The interest rate on a 30 year amortized mortgage is 4.5%. The monthly payment is $1013.37.

At the end of 10 years 81,783.41 in interest paid.

Principal has been reduced $39,820.00.

If you paid $100 a month extra for those 10 years the balance would be reduced by a total of $54.940.84, instead of $39,820.00.

The difference being $15,120.84 more that the mortgage would have paid down.

Taking that same $100 a month and investing it at 5% in 10 years there would be an account of $15,528.23. The mortgage could be paid down by that amount at that point, or just continue to grow the mortgage offset account.

THE ANNUAL CMA (COMPETITIVE MARKET ANALYSIS) FOR CLIENTS 7

I believe that one of the most important services I perform for my clients is an annual CMA on the property they own in my market area. Everyone wants to know what their property is worth! The Annual CMA is simply a report of the activity in the neighborhood that the client's property is located in. By performing this Annual CMA, the opportunity is created to review the value of the client's property and review the Checklist for Real Estate Services to see what other real estate needs the client might have. Clients are often attempting to check their values with various online services. An Annual CMA is another opportunity for the REALTOR® to show their professionalism.

CHECKLIST FOR REAL ESTATE SERVICES

8

As families' needs change, the REALTOR® for life has the opportunity to discuss the variety of services a REALTOR® can offer to provide proper direction for the most appropriate professional help. The general public has no idea of all the services a REALTOR® can help them with throughout their financial life. It is up to us to tell them! The following checklist for real estate services provides a list of topics to talk to your clients about.

LET ME KNOW IF I CAN HELP YOU WITH ANY OF THE FOLLOWING REAL ESTATE SERVICES:

❏ I need a REALTOR® referral to buy or sell real estate in the city of _____.

❏ I would like help towards buying my first home

❏ I would like to investigate the possibility of selling my current home and buying another.

❏ I need to know the market value of my home.

❏ I need to know what to do to get my property ready to sell.

❏ I would like help deciding whether or not to refinance or would like to discuss equity management and mortgage acceleration techniques.

❏ I would like to learn about buying real estate investments for retirement.

❏ I would like to learn about using my IRA or other retirement funds to buy real estate.

❏ I want to check into buying real estate for my child to live in while attending college.

❏ I would like to learn about buying real estate to help save for my child's college education.

❏ I would like to investigate buying a vacation property in ski country, in a tropical setting, or in other resort areas.

- ❑ I need to learn about deferring taxes when I sell my investment property via a 1031 exchange.
- ❑ I would like to exchange my investment into a Tenant in Common (TIC) investment.
- ❑ I need help with estate planning relative to real estate.
- ❑ Other questions.

HELPING YOUR CLIENTS BUY THEIR SECOND (OR THIRD) HOME

9

In most cases, the REALTOR® for Life's next transaction with their client is to help them into their next home. This gives the REALTOR® for life the opportunity to guide the client through the process and discuss the variety of options available for them. I usually use this opportunity to see if they can keep their first home as a rental. Clients are often shocked when I talk about this because they were sure I was just there to list the house, get paid a commission and move on. Regardless of what they decide, it really builds loyalty when you show them you care about their overall financial picture, rather than just listing the house. The following is a list of options to discuss with your clients:

Options when your clients are ready to buy a home but have another home to sell first.

Any time a client is selling one house and buying another there are inherent risks over which you may have no control. Each one of the seven options below has pros and cons. Which Option you pick depends on equity levels, qualifying ratios, etc.

1. Keep the current home as a rental, activate the equity with a refinance, and purchase the new home.

In some cases your client can keep the present home as an investment. It is a good idea for your client to visit with a tax advisor to see if owning an investment property helps his/her tax situation. The general benefits of keeping the property in an investment portfolio include:

- No transaction costs to pay, only refinance costs.

- Tax benefit-depreciation

- Possible future appreciation of the value of the property.

If this alternative is attractive, the next step is to visit with a lender who can determine if your client will qualify for the financing. To qualify for structuring the transaction in this way, the lender will usually consider 75% of the monthly rent to apply toward your income figures, as long as the loan to value ratio is under 75% on the rental property. Any negative cash flow using the formula: Rent x 75% minus monthly PITI (principal, interest, tax, insurance) of the loan secured by the rental, is considered just like any other debt payment and the appropriate ratios applied.

2. List the home conditional upon finding replacement property.
The home can be listed and put it in the comments in the MLS that it is "conditional upon your clients locating a replacement property". This method allows the old home to go under contract, then find a replacement property within an agreed upon period of time. The disadvantage is that some of the best buyers, such as corporate transferees who have three days to buy a house, may not want to look at the house. The reason for this is that they don't want to "wait and see" if they have purchased a house based on your client's ability to find a replacement. In my estimation you lose about 30% of the available buyers by offering the home "conditional upon finding replacement property." If a buyer is willing to purchase the home, "conditional upon finding a replacement property" they will usually give 10 days or so to locate and contract on another one. The difficulty is, what happens if the contract on the home being purchased falls apart after the removal of the condition of "finding replacement property?" A buyer might be willing to wait until contracting on another property but very seldom will wait for resolution of inspection conditions or the actual closing on the "replacement property."

If this option is selected, it is important for you to review the market so that when a contract does come in you can make a quick and informed decision on the purchase of your new home. If this method works it could keep you from doing a double move.

3. Make an offer on a new property conditional upon selling the old property.
It is possible to make an offer on the new home "conditional upon your old home going under contract." This method can also keep you from doing a double move. Our ability to structure the transaction in this way is dependent on market forces. If the market is hot the odds are good that a seller of the home your client wants to buy will receive offers from buyers that do not have a house to sell. In a hot market having a house to sell before you can buy puts you at a negotiating disadvantage.

If it is acceptable for the seller to allow time to sell a house, it is usually structured where your client will have 30 days to get a contract on his/her home and maybe another 60 days to close it. Sometimes when you make an offer conditional upon the old house selling the seller might come back with what is called a "first right of refusal" or more appropriately called a "kick out clause." This means that you and the seller have agreed to the price and terms of the contract. The seller then can continue to market the property and see if they can find a buyer that doesn't need to sell a home. In the event the seller receives another offer to purchase, most first right of refusals have 48 to 72 hours to remove the condition of selling your old home. In order to remove that condition the client would need to have gotten his/her home under contract or arranged for "bridge loan financing."

4. Bridge loan financing

A "bridge loan" will allow clients to activate the equity in their old home to use as down payment for their new home and should be done before putting a house on the market. The advantage of a bridge loan is that it gives the client a strong negotiating position in acquiring a new home by not needing a contingency to sell their current home. A bridge loan will typically allow one to use about 80% of the value of his/her current home, minus the current loan balance for the purchase of a new home. If your client is willing to obtain a bridge loan he/she can "beat out" other buyers who may have a home to sell before they can buy. This method can usually prevent a double move.

The disadvantage of a bridge loan is that if the old house doesn't sell quickly and the client closes on the new home, the client has the new loan payment, the old loan payment, and the bridge loan payment. Often, bridge loans can be structured so that there are no payments of interest due until the house sells or 6 months.

It is also important to remember that bridge loans typically require up front fees that you incur once the loan is closed. For this reason it is normally best to market the home aggressively to try and sell it before needing the bridge and to close on the bridge loan at the last possible moment, if needed. Most lenders will approve clients for the bridge loan up front so that the contingency can be removed. If this alternative appears beneficial, it is in the client's best interest to meet with the lender to determine that qualifying for the bridge loan is likely and to discuss any questions that the client may have.

5. Buy new home using available cash for down payment, a first mortgage in the amount you want to end up with when your old home sells, and a second mortgage on the new home that you will pay off when the old house sells.

The advantage of structuring the transaction in this way is that it gives the negotiating power to purchase the new home and doesn't have a bridge loan's "short fuse." You can avoid mortgage insurance on the first mortgage if you limit it to 80% loan to value. Another alternative is to use available cash for down payment with a maximum mortgage. Then when the old house sells, invest the cash proceeds in other investments.

6. Sell, Move, Buy.
If the client wants to have negotiating power, is willing to do a double move, and can wait for the right home to come along, then sell the old home, move into a temporary situation and watch for the right property to come along. Having the old home sold with the cash in hand, and a pre-approved mortgage gives a strong negotiating position.

7. Shop for a new home, list old home, write contract on new home as soon as old house goes under contract.
The first step in structuring the transaction in this way is to shop and review the market to see if the types of homes the clients are looking for are generally available. Once you have a comfort level, you can put the home on the market. Once there is a contract on the old house you can go write a contract on a new one, conditional upon the old house closing. This puts the client in a negotiating position stronger than having a house to sell, but not as strong as having the cash in the bank or the bridge loan method. To get an offer like this accepted, you need to show the seller of the new home how strong the contract is on the old house.

Generally, if you can show that the buyer is pre-qualified, and it is past the inspection resolution date in the contract, there is a pretty good chance your client can get a contract accepted. If you are able to structure a transaction in this manner the client would try to close on both the old house and the new house on the same day.

WHY BUY UP IN A "DOWN" MARKET?

10

Markets will always cycle up and down! In a "down" market clients often freeze and don't want to take any action. However, that is the time to take action and buy UP in a down market!

Another way to maximize the benefits is to keep the $300,000 house in the above example and rent it. Real estate always cycles and that $300,000 house in this example will go up again. By utilizing the method, in this example, you don't lose the $30,000 and in fact, likely gain from future appreciation and tax benefits.

BUYING "UP" IN A "DOWN" MARKET

A simple example of how this works:

SELL a $300,000 house that has gone down 10%

= $30,000 loss

BUY a $600,000 house that has gone down 10%

= $60,000 gain

Net effect to a buyer is **+ $30,000**

THE REALTOR® FOR LIFE REFERRAL NETWORK

11

One of the ways you remain a client's REALTOR® for Life is helping them with their real estate transactions across the globe! I have been with RE/MAX of Boulder for over 37 years and have attended the RE/MAX International Convention every year! Since that time, RE/MAX has grown across the globe and is now in over 90 countries. I have built a network of 1300 agents where I know their name, face, and city where they work. If you aren't with a global company, you can attend the National Association of REALTORS® convention each year and build your network that way.

In the real estate business, something unique happens! As you build your client base many of them move away to other parts of the world. Most agents lose touch with those clients. A REALTOR® for Life maintains contact! My goal is that no matter where any client moves from or to, they will call me first! I have had a client move from Boulder to Maryland. When it came time to move from Maryland to Texas, they called me for a referral in each of those cities because they knew that I knew someone personally! I have another client with five kids, now adults. Those "kids" have moved all over the country and always call me first for a referral.

As a REALTOR® for Life, you need to know from where people are relocating to your city. As a REALTOR® you can go on www.realtor.org to get a relocation report that shows you where people are coming from. I use this information to determine which cities I need to spend the most time to maintain contact with those REALTORS®. It also gives me a focus on what REALTORS®, from which cities, are most important to meet.

In my market in Boulder, Colorado, people love to buy nearby ski area condos and vacation in a variety of island locations! I maintain close contact with REALTORS® in those favorite spots.

Boulder is also a college town. I'm sorry to say, not everyone who grows up in Boulder decides to attend the University of Colorado. That gives me the opportunity to refer my clients to REALTORS® in other college towns so that they can buy a college condo for their student in that town.

The bottom line is, your clients want to work with someone they can trust. Building a referral network across the globe truly provides an excellent service to your client base.

HELP YOUR CLIENTS INVEST IN REAL ESTATE! 12

Why invest in real estate?

I would say that most people consider their single family home they live in as an investment in real estate and in fact when they fill out a financial statement it is even listed as an asset. It's true that the home will likely go up in value over the years and as the loan is paid off it could be a large part of a person's net worth. However, in the truest sense of the word, the personal residence is really a liability rather than an investment. Think about it! On your home you have a mortgage payment, taxes, utilities, maintenance, etc. It all adds up to a pretty good amount of money going out each month, with no money coming into the equation from the property. It really is a liability! Now, think of a little single family rental! If you have an amortizing mortgage on it and the rent pays the mortgage and expenses, each month you build equity via principal reduction. Eventually, rents go up and the property becomes free and clear and it produces cash flow that you can use to go to the store and buy groceries.

Potential for appreciation

Residential real estate has proven to be a good investment over the years. Over the long term values have continued to rise in my home market of Boulder County. However, there certainly have been times when market conditions have slowed sales and prices dipped. An old saying says, "Buy real estate and wait." In Boulder County, if you bought in the 1980s, you would have bought and waited. In the 1990's appreciation was much stronger and a profit could be made after only waiting a short time.

Job Growth Drives Appreciation

The primary reason appreciation occurs is job growth. If job growth is occurring, new families move and need a place to live. When job growth stops, the real estate market levels off. Job growth is even more important than interest rate levels on the overall market. Lower interest rates will stimulate the local move-up market. If someone doesn't have a job, it probably doesn't matter what the interest rate is.

Debt Reduction

Every month when a payment is made on the mortgage, a certain amount goes toward principal reduction. If one of the goals is to have free and clear real estate, a payment schedule can be created on a 30-year loan that will pay off the loan in whatever time frame desired. In most cases the rent is paying for the mortgage payment. Each month that goes by, the tenant is helping pay off the loan and build equity.

Leverage

The concept of leverage is what is known as using "other people's money" or OPM. When investing in real estate, it makes the most sense to get a loan for a good portion of the purchase price. To illustrate an example of leverage, lets say you had $100,000 to invest. You then used that money to purchase one $100,000 condominium. If the real estate market were appreciating at 5% a year and you held the property for 5 years the condominium would be worth $122,347 or a gain of $22,347. Now lets say that instead, you took that same $100,000, put $20,000 down on each of 5 $100,000 condominiums. You now own $500,000 worth of real estate. If it appreciates at the same 5% a year for 5 years it would be worth $638,140 or a gain of $138,140 on the same $100,000 investment. As you trade up, it is important to keep your equity position at a level that allows you to survive downturns in the rental market.

Tax Break

Everyone should consult a tax advisor on how ownership of real estate will affect them personally. The 1986 Tax Reform took away many of the major benefits of owning real estate and made real estate "pay for itself." Today, there is no "doubling declining depreciation!" We still have depreciation, but it is subject to income limits and other rules. Depending on how someone fits in with the IRS rules, they could potentially get a tax break for its depreciation. Depreciation is a tax concept whereby you get a write off but don't have to spend the actual dollars to get it. For example, on a $100,000 purchase, an accountant may choose to declare 80% of the value as depreciable. You can't declare the whole value as depreciable because some of the value is attributed to land and land doesn't "depreciate." Therefore, in this example, $80,000 would be depreciable. Under the current IRS rules, you can take the $80,000 and divide it by 27.5 years for an annual depreciation deduction of about $2,900. In addition to depreciation, real estate taxes and other expenses of the property can offset rental income. The bottom line is that real estate, in the early years of ownership, will show a loss, which results in a tax deduction and tax savings. There are limits as to the amounts that can be deducted due to real estate losses. Depreciation can also be "recaptured" at time of sale, which means that there is a higher taxable gain. You need to consult a tax advisor to determine how all the IRS rules will affect someone personally.

Cash Flow

In the early years of ownership, it is difficult to achieve immediate positive cash flow with which can be taken to spend at the grocery store. In other words, when a property is first purchased, the rental income probably won't cover the mortgage payment and all the expenses. If the cash flow is about break-even on a month-to-month basis, after taxes and appreciation factors are considered, the overall cash flow is positive. After owning the property for several years, rents should go up, the mortgage payment stays the same (except for increases in taxes and insurance), and the monthly cash flow increases.

Liquidity-Conversion to cash

Real Estate is not a "liquid" investment compared to many other investments available. If someone needed to sell a property to generate cash, market conditions will dictate how marketable a particular property will be. Generally speaking, individual housing units, whether single family or condo, have been readily salable in our marketplace. However, one does not need to sell a property in order to generate cash. If you have owned the property for a while and its equity has increased, you can refinance your loan to pull cash out. With refinancing, you don't have to pay any selling expenses or pay any tax on the cash pulled out. The money can be used for daily expenses, other investments, or for the down payment on another rental property.

Single Family for appreciation

In my marketplace in Boulder, Colorado, the rents compared to the value don't make much sense. So why do people still buy them as investments? They hope that the appreciation rate will cause the value of their house to increase so much that the monthly cash flow may not be important to a particular investor.

Multi-units for cash flow

Typically a single-family residence will have a higher gross rent multiplier. The gross rent multiplier is simply the annual gross rent compared to the purchase price. The lower the gross rent multiplier, the greater the return for the dollar invested. The greater the number of units in a building, the lower the gross rent multiplier typically is.

When trading a single-family for multi-units you usually won't see much change when moving up to a 4-unit. The best increases in cash flow comes when making the jump to 20-plus units in one location.

Comparing residential real estate to other possible investments

Residential real estate investment can be for almost anyone. The first real estate purchase can typically be made without a lot of capital or experience.

Stock Market

The stock market has tended to have many more ups and downs than the real estate market. The stock market is a gamble for most passive investors. As an experienced and knowledgeable investor there are certainly opportunities to make money. Every time stocks have a downturn, investors often turn to real estate because it is typically a more stable investment. It is possible to use leverage in the stock market by purchasing on "margin." However, if the stock turns down in value there will just be debt to pay.

Savings Accounts

Savings accounts are a great, safe place to save money, but as an investment, typically taxes on the income and the rate of inflation offset any gains from the interest payment.

Gold and Silver

For the knowledgeable investor there are certainly opportunities to make money. Again, for the passive investor, the market is very risky.

Vacant Land

Buying land in the path of progress is a great idea. However, while you're waiting for progress to catch up, holding costs, such as debt service, taxes, etc., can eat up future return on the investment.

Commercial Real Estate

Commercial tenants have specialized needs. Often when a commercial tenant moves out the entire interior of the building needs to be redone. If a large commercial tenant moves out it could take a considerable period of time to re-lease the property.

Comparing one real estate investment to another

There are several rules of thumb that help you compare different investment properties. The perfect comparison would account for all factors involved in a real estate investment:

- Rent amounts

- Purchase price

- Initial investment

- Appreciation

- Depreciation

- Expenses

- Loan amount

- Holding period

- Time value of money

- Exact future sales price and tax liability upon sale

None of the following methods are "perfect" comparisons; they all have their advantages and disadvantages.

Gross Rent Multiplier (GRM)

The most commonly used rule of thumb is called the gross rent multiplier. It simply compares the price of the property to the annual gross rent. Part of the reason it is so popular as a rule of thumb is that on each listing sheet in our local Multiple Listing Service (MLS) for income property, a GRM is calculated by the computer and shown on the listing sheet. In general, the lower the GRM, the better the value is to the investor. Its drawback is that it only considers rent and price out of all the factors in the bulleted list above.

Capitalization Rate (Cap Rate)

This is popular because it is also easy to compute. It is arrived at by dividing the Net Operating Income by the price. It is also indicated on our local MLS sheet for each property. In theory, it is a better measure than the GRM because it considers the Net Operating Income (rent less the expenses of the property). The problem is that the expenses of the property are rarely reflected accurately in the MLS and often not accurate even when they come directly from the owner. If the expenses are in error, and the MLS computer calculates the cap rate, you have garbage in, garbage out. Therefore, for this rule of thumb to have the most meaning to an individual investor, it is best to try to figure out what expenses are exact for each property and add realistic estimates for total expenses for each property analyzed.

Cash on Cash

Cash on Cash is one of the easiest to compare directly to a more liquid investment. Simply take the annual cash flow after expenses but before taxes and divide it by the initial investment. The result is a percent return that you can compare to the investment where the cash is sitting prior to investing in real estate. The drawback is that it only considers rent, expenses, and initial investment out of all the factors in the bulleted list on page 30.

Debt Coverage Ratio

When applying for a loan on a multi-unit or 5+ unit, most lenders will consider a ratio called the debt coverage ratio. This ratio compares Net Operating Income to the Principal and Interest payment. Lenders will typically want to see a ratio of 1.2+. Another way to look at it is the NOI must be 120% of the monthly principal and interest payment. Lenders will be using their own formula for computing NOI. Sometimes the biggest variance will be in an estimate for expenses and vacancy allowances.

Internal Rate of Return (IRR)

Probably the best comparison of all, used by the most serious investors, but in general probably used the least because it is the hardest to calculate. This comparison considers many more of the factors listed above, but its accuracy is limited by the accuracy of expense information available, correct mortgage figures, accuracy of prediction of future cash flows (rents and future sales price), accuracy of predicted investor tax bracket at time of sale, etc. Even though the theory behind all of the IRR is great, it's still just a guess on how the property might perform in the future.

The best example of how inaccurate it might be is the appreciation factor. Lets say in your analysis of past data the appreciation rate has been 8% a year. Just after purchasing it, the real estate market slows and the appreciation rate is actually 4% per year over the ownership period. The difference between those two numbers significantly affects the IRR. Using IRR does provide a great opportunity to put "real numbers" into the formula after the property has been owned for five years, sold, and the taxes paid. With those "real numbers" one can can truly compare a real estate investment to other investments that competed for the investment dollar five years ago. For more information and to purchase a program to easily calculate IRR, go to landlordsoftware.com.

DUANE'S TOP 10 INVESTING TIPS

13

1 **Have a goal and a plan.**
It can be as simple as "buy one house per year."

2 **Buy HOUSES for APPRECIATION.**
Buy MULTI-UNITS for CASH FLOW.

3 **Buy Real Estate and Wait**
As opposed to "I could have bought that for…"

4 **Never Sell**
- As opposed to "I shouldn't have sold that for…" Do 1031 Exchanges instead
- Never Say Never! Unless…
- Sometimes it might actually make sense to sell a property, pay the tax, and buy another. The reason might be that you get a higher depreciable basis to shelter current income.

5 **Assemble your investment team**
- REALTOR®
- 1-4 unit lender
- 5+ unit lender
- CPA
- Attorney
- Insurance agent
- Exchange Company
- Self Directed IRA Company
- Tenant in Common (TIC) Company

- Title Company
- Property Manager
- Service contacts for fix up

6 Pay off loans early or not?

7 Hire a manager

8 Educate yourself
- Be able to evaluate quickly
- Think outside your own market area
- Stick to what you know

9 Leverage

10 Do it
Some people look for the "perfect" investment for so long they never end up doing anything!

REAL ESTATE AS A COLLEGE SAVINGS ACCOUNT
14

Buying a rental property when a baby is born is a great way to save for college. If one buys a rental property with a 15-year mortgage when the child is born it will be paid off with 3 years to go when the child turns 18 and goes to college. It could be sold, the taxes paid, and used as cash for college. One could refinance to pull cash out, tax-free and use the cash for college. One could keep it free and clear and just use the monthly cash flow to pay for college expenses. In many cases in my market, the student actually will use the house to live in during college and rent it out to roommates.

Hindsight is always perfect, but, for example, if someone bought a home in the Baseline subdivision, in my marketplace in Boulder, CO, just east of the university, in 1996 when a child was born one would have paid about $170,000. Now when the child turned 18 in 2013 the home was worth about $350,000 and you have no loan on it. You can use the money as stated in the above options. Right now those homes rent for about $1500 to $1800 a month. You would need to pay taxes and insurance and maintenance expenses and the remaining cash flow could go toward monthly college expenses.

In the early years of the 15-year mortgage, there probably won't be enough rent to cover the whole mortgage payment. One might investigate other financing options, such as the 30-year mortgage, to help with cash flow in the early years of ownership, but then use mortgage acceleration techniques to be sure it is free and clear by the time college starts.

BUYING A NEW HOME AS AN INVESTMENT $\mathbf{15}$

The new home market seems to have wider fluctuations than the typical resale market. In some markets, builders have had lotteries to determine which buyer would be able to pick a lot on which to build a home. If a market slows down, builders will often offer thousands of dollars of incentives to get buyers to buy.

As an investor, there are many advantages to buying a new home:

1. A new home has less maintenance issues and usually comes with a warranty.

2. A new home is usually easier to rent since it has all the latest features that people want.

3. When you buy in a new home subdivision, and the builder has sold out, the value of the home often appreciates.

4. At the end of almost every year, builders are anxious to get any standing inventory off the books. Often they will have very large incentives if a buyer can close before the end of the year.

5. In an appreciating market, if you contract on a dirt start, you can lock in the price without having to close for 6-8 months. By the time you close the value of the property is likely to be higher than the price paid.

6. There are often attractive financing packages offered by the builder.

7. Not all new home subdivisions allow investors.

CREATING WEALTH THROUGH REAL ESTATE WHILE YOU SLEEP!

16

Or playing Monopoly in real life!
How many things can one do that creates wealth while they sleep? Real estate is exciting because every night when you go to bed, you have rental income coming in, values increasing over time, loan balances declining with every monthly payment and possible tax benefits. I love keeping track of how much principal reduction I have each month on my investment portfolio!

Rental Income Coming In
As long as you have the properties with good features, in good locations, leased with deposits and screened tenants, you can be fairly comfortable that the rent will continue to come in every month. Starting out, if you are highly leveraged, there may not be much immediate cash flow to be able to use to buy food at the grocery store. However, part of the plan is to get debt paid down and then rents do go up over time!

Values Increasing Over Time = Appreciation

While this is being written in 2015, we are coming out of some tough times in many markets across the county. However, looking at the long-term performance of the appreciation of real estate values in the United States, it has been good over time.

The very rapid appreciation of the 2000's was certainly not sustainable, and in 2009 to 2012 many areas of the country suffered a hard crash. In my 30-plus-year career, I have seen several cycles. Real Estate will cycle up again AND it will cycle down again. Part of the purpose of this book is to learn to create a real estate portfolio that can withstand the inevitable ups and downs of any real estate market. Today, there is a website at www.fhfa.gov where you can study the rise and fall of hundreds of real estate markets across the country.

Many people are asking today if real estate will ever recover. In some areas of the country it will take a while. There are many factors that will fuel the next cycle:

1. Population continues to increase by births.

2. Population increases in some areas by migration and/or immigration.

3. Lack of new construction.

4. Pent-up demand of households living in parents' basements, foreclosed and short sale owners that will once again want to be a homeowner.

5. New jobs as the economy improves.

6. Credit standards relaxing as the economy improves.

In my own portfolio, it's safe to say, I have realized an average of 5% increase in values of real estate I have owned long term. Each night when I go to sleep, I rest comfortably with the feeling that my well-located real estate will sustain and increase its value and as each month goes by I get closer to a free and clear real estate portfolio!

LOAN BALANCES DECLINE WITH EVERY MONTHLY PAYMENT

I think this is one of the most exciting parts of owning investment real estate! Each month you get rent from a tenant that makes your mortgage payment. Each month the loan balance goes down. Early on in a 30-year mortgage, the principal reduction is relatively small. But as each month goes by, the principal reduction gets bigger and bigger. As loans get older it is pretty fun to calculate how much your equity increases in the form of debt reduction every day.

POSSIBLE TAX BENEFITS

Prior to 1986, an investor could buy enough real estate to eliminate a tax bill. Double declining depreciation could melt away a tax bill with the fury of 1000 jungle beasts. After 1986, real estate was pretty much forced to pay for itself rather than be purchased solely for the tax benefits. Now, the depreciation benefit is still a factor, but it phases out as income rises. Each investor needs to consult their own tax expert to determine how owning investment real estate will affect them. There are increased tax benefits for those that qualify as a "real estate professional."

REAL ESTATE PROFESSIONAL TAX STATUS

High income tax payers are typically not able to use all of their passive losses from real estate. As a real estate professional, you may qualify for a special tax status that allows you to take full advantage of losses from real estate, that otherwise might be limited. If you are a full time real estate broker, and work at least 750 hours in that capacity, it is likely you will meet the requirement. Meet with your tax professional to determine if you qualify and how it might affect you.

Let's get to work on a plan so that you too can earn money while you sleep.

It can be a simple plan, such as buy one house a year for ten years. When I got started in real estate, it was pretty much assumed that real estate would always go up in value. After the 2000s, we know that may not always be true. But let's take a look at this idea that works when the market appreciates over a 10-year period of time.

1. Buy one house a year for ten years.

2. At the end of year ten, pull cash out by refinancing the house bought in year one, to the extent the rent pays for the mortgage. The cash pulled out is tax-free because pulling cash out from a refinance is not taxable.

3. At the end of year 11, pull cash out by refinancing the house bought in year two.

4. Repeat the process until year 20 and start over.

Works great as long as values rise, rents rise, and financing is available when you need it.

A More Conservative Approach
1. Set a goal

2. Desired income goal derived from investment rental houses $_____

3. To obtain that income if each house has a net rental income of $_____, the number of houses I must own free and clear is _____.

4. The houses will be free and clear by the year _____.

Goals are set, now what?

You need a down payment! Where to get it?
1. **SAVINGS** If there isn't any, start skipping the morning latte, iron your own shirts, wash your own car, sell the new car and

get a free and clear used one! Start building your savings.

2. **SELL** Stock, mutual funds, any other financial investments. If none, go back to step one.

3. **PULL MONEY FROM YOUR RETIREMENT ACCOUNT** or purchase in your retirement account. If none, go back to step one.

4. **REFINANCE** personal residence or other properties to pull cash out. If none, go back to step one.

5. Get a **SECOND JOB** with all earnings going into your real estate investment fund.

You get the idea; if you make a conscious effort you can skip a few luxuries and save money fast.

PURCHASING THAT MULTI-UNIT BUILDING

17

Why purchase Multi-unit buildings instead of single family?

I started investing in single-family homes. Once they were free and clear, I used them for down payments on multi-unit 1031 Exchanges. Here are the advantages to purchasing multi-units:

Cash flow!

The main reason is monthly cash flow. As the number of units increase in one building, the gross rent multiplier (gross rent for the year compared to the purchase price or GRM) typically will go down. When a multiplier goes down, the monthly cash flow will go up. The GRM is just a quick and dirty method to analyze a building. It does not take into account things such as owner-paid utilities etc., but often will eliminate a building from consideration immediately, because it isn't even close to being at market value.

Efficiency

Compare buying a 25 unit to 25 single-family homes or condos. To buy 25 condos or houses you would need 25 loans, 25 appraisals, 25 insurance policies, 25 closings etc. In other words, it is much easier to buy one 25 unit building than it is to buy 25 individual properties. Then once you own it, management is so much easier for 25 units in one place than to manage 25 single-family homes or condos.

Shopping for a multi-unit property

As you shop for a multiunit you are seldom allowed to see all units before writing a contract. Usually just a couple units are shown. After you write a contract, you can usually get into all units during the inspection or appraisal. There are also cases where an owner will not allow you to see units at all until you write a contact conditional upon inspection. Getting all the numbers from an owner for you to analyze is often difficult. Experience will help you quickly determine if an owner's numbers are realistic and what realistic projections will be.

Listing Information Exchanges (aka MLS):

The system for marketing multi-units is much different than residential property. The apartment brokerage community can seem very fragmented, sometimes within their own offices. This is due to the fact that many multifamily brokers track their own databases of owners and often know the likely buyer(s) when they gain a new listing. Therefore, sometimes the most efficient activity is for that broker to approach a likely buyer directly. Locally there is a commercial REALTOR board called DMCAR, which stands for (Denver Metropolitan Commercial Association of REALTORS). Many commercial brokers belong to this trade organization, and some of them will list their properties in DMCAR's affiliate website (currently Xceligent.com). The majority of DMCAR's agents use either LoopNet, CoStar, or both websites to publicly offer their listings for sale. There area also many brokerage firms that will list properties on their own websites before advertising their listings on the aforementioned information exchanges. Whichever market you participate in, you should research and get to know some of the "heavy hitters" in the multifamily sales niche.

The contract

In Colorado, the contract to purchase a multiunit building is the same as single family as long as it does not exceed 4 units. Once the 5-unit threshold is reached, the contract is a commercial contract, rather than a residential contract. A number of additional provisions are usually used to allow for due diligence.

Ownership

It is never a good idea to own an apartment building personally. Too many things can happen that you should limit your liability. This is done by creating an entity such as a Limited Liability Company (LLC). Apartment owners with multiple buildings might have an LLC for each building and may even form a Limited Liability Limited Partnership (LLLP) that owns all the LLCs. It is best to consult an attorney and CPA to determine which form of ownership works for you. Once you determine what form of ownership works for you, the next step is to coordinate with the lender's requirements. Some lenders will let you buy in the name of the LLC and other's will not. If they won't let you sign initially in the name of an LLC, you can work with your attorney to transfer title to the LLC later, for liability protection.

Financing

Financing for 5+ multi-units is completely different than financing for single-family homes and condos. In fact, the lenders are different and the source of funding for apartment financing is different. Typically there are no 30-year fixed rate mortgages, but different forms of adjustable mortgages are available. Closing costs can vary substantially between lenders. It is very important to shop around and create a relationship with a lender prior to making a purchase.

Quick rules of thumb that lenders and buyers look at:

Debt Coverage Ratio
In single family financing the buyer's ability to repay is the paramount issue. In multi-family, the lender is looking more at how the property will perform and its ability to pay back the loan. One of the primary rules of thumb used is what is called the debt coverage ratio. The debt coverage ratio is determined by taking the annual rent less all the annual expenses. That number needs to be 1.2 times (or 120% of) the total debt service for the year.

Vacancy
A vacancy rate, based on the lender's experience, is used in the calculation of the debt coverage ratio above. Often, the vacancy rate in some market conditions will substantially change the loan to value that a lender might be willing to do. In addition, a lender might not allow closing with a large number of vacancies.

Capitalization Rate (referred to as the CAP rate)
The CAP rate is simply the net operating income from the property divided by the sales price. Net operating income is defined as gross income less total operating expenses and vacancy.

Cash on Cash Return
This is the cash return after annual expenses and debt service is paid divided by the amount of cash investment made.

Appraisals
Appraisals are much more expensive than in the single-family world. However, remember, when buying a 25-unit, it is still much cheaper than doing 25 individual single-family appraisals. The individual multi-unit appraisal contains a very detailed analysis of the "income approach" to value. In other words, the income is what creates the value for an apartment building!

A, B, C, and D Buildings
These are classifications generally used in the apartment industry. In general, class A is at the newer end of the scale and D are the older end of the scale. Class A units typically don't have many opportunities to create new value because they are already in great

shape and there is nothing more to be done. Class B and C (10 to 30 year old buildings) will typically have the greatest opportunities to add value. Class D can also have opportunities, but it takes more intensive due diligence to make sure you are avoiding major structural, electrical or plumbing problems.

Inspections

Part of your contract to purchase a multi-unit building will give an opportunity to do inspections before closing on the property. Some of these inspections might just be the smart thing to do and others may be required by the lender. It is wise to know what tests your lender will typically require so you have a good idea as to what expenses there will be. Remember, inspectors are paid regardless of whether or not you complete the transaction, but if they find a "show stopper" they are worth every penny.

The first inspection is usually a general inspection. The general inspector will go through all the units and look at all aspects of the building. Some parts of the building will likely require a specialist. Those areas might be for things such as the boiler or roof.

You may want to have the property checked for lead-based paint, asbestos, aluminum wiring, pests, environmental items and a variety of other issues.

Insurance

Just like financing for the multi-unit building, insurance for the multi-unit building is a specialty. Before buying a building you want to become familiar with insurance agents that offer commercial insurance. Apartment insurance quotes can vary widely for the same coverage. Insurance is part of an overall protection package, along with your form of ownership.

Apartment policies typically will include a few unique features, such as a code enforcement provision. For instance, if you have an older building and it burns down, the new codes may be different than the code when the building was built. An example might be where now 10 parking spaces are required for the building and a parking garage needs to be built underneath the building as you rebuild it.

Closing day

The closing day for a multi unit building takes the same basic format as a closing for a house. However, there are a few unique items, such as assignment of leases, tenant estoppels, the pro-ration of rents, and the transfer of security deposits.

Management

Professional management is a must for the multiunit building. An individual could do their own management but a professional will get better rents, better deposits and will do a much better job at screening the tenants. In addition, a large property manager can usually help you keep control of expenses by having several of their own maintenance people on staff. In a large building, some might even have a resident manager to help with day-to-day duties.

A professional manager is also able to stay up to date on new laws and trends affecting property owners that an individual owner may never even know about. A great example is the Lead Base Paint Disclosure. The owner is required to give a Lead-Based Paint Disclosure with any leases of apartments in buildings built prior to 1978, whether lead based paint was ever used or not. Many individual owners that I see have never done this. The fines are substantial!

Because all the units are grouped together, typically the management fee for a 25 unit building, as a percentage, will be less than the management fee for 25 individual homes.

Laundry

Multi-unit buildings will often have a common laundry facility. These machines are seldom owned by the owner of the building. They are usually provided by a service such as Automatic Laundry. Automatic Laundry will service the machines, collect the revenues, and pay the building owner a commission. Laundry companies will often have long term contracts that may transfer with the building upon purchase. Laundry contracts should be reviewed along with all the other due diligence items.

Expenses

Sellers of buildings will often deliver an expense report to the prospective buyer. These reports should be reviewed with a complete realistic analysis being done of expenses based both on the current owner's numbers and a projection of future expenses based on current trends.

A seller's report should include entries for the following:
- Interest
- Principal
- Taxes
- Insurance
- Water
- Sewer

- Common Utilities such as common boiler or lighting
- Management
- Advertising
- Legal
- Snow removal and lawn care
- Regular Maintenance and supplies
- Make unit ready for new tenant expenses
- Vacancy
- Accounting
- Misc.

BUYING A PROPERTY TO FIX UP
18

Over the years I have had many clients come to me with the thought of "fixing and flipping." Many people think of taking a run down property, doing some fix-up and making a huge profit. In reality, you need to analyze each project carefully to make sure there is room to make a profit at all. There is risk in investing in real estate and doing renovations, but this chapter will help you manage that risk.

Fix-up properties can range from buying a 1,000 square foot ranch and updating the basic systems or doing a major remodel with a "pop top". The time and money it takes to renovate the property and the time it will take to sell the property are critical factors in whether or not you make a profit in your fix-up venture. The fix up expenses will be the same regardless of what you pay for the property. The key to success is buying right!

Part of the plan should include determining the goals: to buy, fix-up and hold or buy, fix-up, and sell immediately. If you are doing larger properties they usually don't make much sense as rentals, so those you usually want to sell immediately. A less expensive property may make a great rental to keep for a while and then trade if for a larger investment property.

Team Members for your clients to assemble
- REALTOR®
- CPA
- Attorney
- Title Company
- Inspector
- Insurance Agent
- Short Term Lender
- Long Term Lender
- Contractor list
- Supplier list

"FIXER-UPPER" COST ANALYSIS

Analyze major components of house and the cost to repair or upgrade

Roof	$_____
Furnace	$_____
Siding	$_____
Windows	$_____
Flooring	$_____
Landscaping	$_____
Plumbing	$_____
Wiring	$_____
Demolition and haul off	$_____

Analyze other fix-up expenses

Carpet	$_____
Kitchen and bath flooring	$_____
Paint	$_____
Kitchen cabinets, counters	$_____
Bathroom cabinets, counters	$_____
Appliances	$_____
Holding period expenses	$_____
Interest on financing for holding period	$_____
Taxes for holding period	$_____
Utilities for holding period	$_____

TOTAL: $_____

Will your clients do the work themselves or hire contractors?

If they have the skills and the time to do much of the work themselves, they have the opportunity to build "sweat equity". However, most people will need to hire someone to do any fix-up work. If you need to hire someone, it is critical to your project to use a team of reputable contractors.

Be sure to get all bids in writing and a performance agreement as to the time the work will be done. Don't be lured into getting a cheaper price by not getting a permit. If the work requires a permit be sure to get one. Otherwise, when you go to sell and the buyer asks for one, getting a retro active permit can be a real problem.

Time is Money

This old saying couldn't be any truer than in doing fix and flips. The whole team needs to be assembled to take action as soon as possible the day the property is purchased. If you are borrowing money to purchase, each day that goes by cuts into the potential profits.

Market analysis for resale

Investigate and go look at properties that have been fixed up and find out what their sale prices were. You will get ideas as to what type of fix-up helps the property to sell, and at what price. Analyze the time of year that your property will come available. Is the market strong when your fix-up is ready to sell?

NET PROCEEDS EVALUATION

Time to sell your fixed-up property and evaluate your net proceeds:

Purchase price	$_____
Title insurance	$_____
Real estate brokerage	$_____
Loan payoff	$_____
Pro-rated interest	$_____
Loan release fee	$_____
Courier fee for payoff	$_____
Water escrow	$_____
Closing fee	$_____
Tax proration	$_____
Any seller paid buyer closing costs	$_____
Any buyer inspection items	$_____
Net proceeds	$_____
Tax Effects	$_____
Profit after taxes	$_____

Other areas to investigate:
- Tax Credits for Rehab of Historic Structures
- Tax Credits for Low-income housing
- If it is an owner occupied renovation, visit with your tax professional to determine if you can get favorable tax treatment if you live in the property two out of five years.

Selling process

If the property is left vacant while it is for sale, it is good to at least stage the property to a certain extent. This could be as simple as putting a few kitchen and bath items in and possibly furnish one bedroom and the living room.

Another option is to use a company such as Showhomes of America. The idea behind this concept is putting someone in the house and keeping it "Showhome Ready." There is no fee charged to the owner of the property. The Showhome tenant pays rent to Showhomes at a reduced rate. They agree to keep the property ready for showings at all times. The Showhome tenant will typically pay for utilities and maintain the yard.

Finding the property

The price of the property in a certain area will usually dictate whether or not it is a fix-up property.

Fix-up Minor or Major?

Watch out for the major problems-such as foundation and structural issues. Major problems can quickly wipe out any potential profit.

- Have a professional inspection done
- Get an inspection of the major components of the house

Other due diligence:

- Determine if the property is in the flood plain. If the property is in the flood plain a lender would require flood insurance and it could make it more difficult to sell.

- Can the property be insured? Have your insurance agent look at the house and run a CLUE report on it and yourself.

- Picking the right neighborhood

- Is another fix-up being done?

- Check schools, shopping, any other services?

- Check crime rate?

- Purchase price of the property

- Once you find a property, you can analyze the cost to fix-up and value after fix-up to determine the maximum you can pay and still make a profit.

- In addition to Fix-up expenses you will have acquisition costs, selling expenses and taxes if you make a profit.

Acquisition expenses for a permanent loan
- Loan fees
- Appraisal
- Tax service fee
- Title Insurance for lender
- Tax certificate
- Recording fees
- State doc fee
- Insurance
- Misc. Lender fees
- Interest proration
- Tax and Insurance Reserves
- Short term Commercial Loans

Sometimes it is more economical to make an arrangement with a commercial banker to provide short term financing while the property is being renovated. With a short-term commercial loan, one would hopefully have the home resold before the loan comes due. This way you would never have to put a permanent loan on the property.

Make the potential buyer say "WOW" as they walk in the door. Almost every buyer that says "WOW" when they walk in the door will end up buying the house. Therefore, your goal should be to make them say "WOW" from the curb and then again as they walk in the front door. What will it take to give the maximum amount of curb appeal? What will it take to make the kitchen and bath "sizzle?" What will it take to make the house light and bright?

Options for financing the fix up property
1. Pay cash for property and cash for fix up
2. Pay cash for property, short-term loan for improvements
3. Short term loan to purchase, possibly borrow for construction expenses
4. Permanent loan to keep and hold
5. Permanent Mortgage to purchase, cash for improvements
6. Buy with a short-term loan, fix up, hold a year, and then exchange for other property
7. Some lenders will only refinance based on purchase price until a year goes by.
8. You need to know what your lender's requirements are.
9. Owner occupied renovation financing is definitely easier to obtain, with programs such as the FHA 203k program.

ADDING VALUE TO AN APARTMENT BUILDING AFTER YOU HAVE PURCHASED IT

19

An apartment building goes up in value based on the income derived from the building. Anything you can do to create a track record of an increased income stream will help you in selling the building or justifying value if you choose to refinance.

The following is a list of brainstorming ideas for increasing the value of a building:

1. **Increase rents.** This can be accomplished by improving management or improving the property. In slow times, as rents fall, it is important to keep the building full

2. **Market your unit**
   - List with any local rental listing service or web site.
   - Make a brochure and place in a brochure box on property. Use pictures so a prospective tenant can see how nice the units are.
   - Use incentives to current tenants to refer new tenants to you.
   - Send a thank you to existing tenants. Include a couple movie tickets.

2. **Expense control**
   - Water - stop all leaks, low flow toilets and shower heads
   - Insurance - review insurance annually for the most competitive policy
   - Gas - If owner pays gas bill- get more efficient boiler, better windows
   - Property tax review - appeal if comparable sales show a lower value
   - Trash - review for a more competitive price each year

3. Convert a master-metered property to a sub-metered property transferring utility expense to tenants

4. Accurate records-Accurate rent rolls and expense figures help the buyer obtain financing more readily.

5. Improve the property
   - Increase the curb appeal
   - Provide clean and comfortable laundry area
   - Provide adequate mail area
   - Put in bike racks
   - Upgrade wiring or plumbing if necessary to obtain future financing

6. Add coin operated laundry, pop machines.

7. Add storage areas or garages or convert storage area to rentable living space.

8. Charge cable or satellite companies for the right to install in the building.

9. Provide access to rooftop for cellular phone antenna.

10. Buy the building next door to increase efficiency of management.

11. Check into low interest rate improvement loans that may be offered by a city for targeted rehab areas.

12. Increase Security by fencing or using a buzzer system.

13. Investigate Condo Conversion potential.

1031 REAL ESTATE EXCHANGES

20

When most people hear the words 1031 Exchange they think it would be difficult to do because "who would want to exchange directly with me?" The IRS, in Section 1031 of the tax code, has outlined specific guidelines for creating a 1031 Exchange of real estate.

If you are an owner of investment real estate and want to continue to climb the investment ladder, a 1031 Exchange could be just the ticket for you. The 1031 Exchange allows you to continue your investment in real estate, while deferring taxes on any gain, so that you can climb the investment ladder faster.

What is a 1031 Exchange?

A 1031 Exchange is a transaction where the IRS allows you to sell a real estate investment, replace it with another, without paying tax on the gain of the first property at the time of sale. This tax concept allows you to keep trading up without having to write a check to the government each time you trade up. Sometimes these exchanges are called "tax free" but they are actually "tax deferred". Tax is finally paid when you no longer want to be a real estate investor and are ready to "cash out". To qualify for a 1031 Exchange there is a list of requirements, with which most are easy to comply.

General Rules for a 1031 Exchange

The current rule reads that upon closing the sale of the first property the owner has 45 days to locate the exchange property and 180 days to close on it. Therefore, it is wise to talk with both your CPA and your REALTOR® before selling and closing on your property. If 45 days after the closing of the sale of your old property you don't have an exchange property selected, your exchange will be disallowed and tax will be due. That 45 days can pass very quickly.

The "Like Kind" rule of section 1031 of the code states that the properties exchanged must be like kind. This simply means that the investment must continue in real estate. For example, if you own vacant land, you can exchange it for an improved income producing property such as an apartment building or an office building.

Must be qualifying property. Qualifying property is property held for investment or used in a taxpayer's trade or business.

Any 'boot' received will be taxable. Boot is any property which is not like kind. If the seller desires some cash or debt reduction this is okay as long the seller realizes some tax will be due. You don't want to receive any boot if you want the transaction to be 100% tax deferred. A rule of thumb to defer taxes is to always replace the exchange property with one of equal or greater value and debt.

You should bring cash to the closing of the Exchange Property to cover charges, which are not transaction costs, such as utility escrows, rent pro-rations, etc. An Exchange Intermediary must be used to hold the exchange funds from the closing of the old property.

The Exchange intermediary
In the typical exchange you will be selling a property that you have been holding for investment. According to the IRS rules you cannot touch the money that comes from the closing of your former property. You need to hire what is called an Exchange Intermediary. The Intermediary will charge a fee for doing the Exchange Agreement and all the necessary paperwork. The Intermediary will hold your cash proceeds until you are ready to close on the replacement investment property.

The Exchange agreement
The agreement between the investor and the Exchange Intermediary contains an assignment of the contract to the intermediary. It allows the intermediary to hold the funds until the next closing. If the investor were to take receipt of the funds a taxable event would occur. The deadlines for the identification and closing of property will be specified. It will allow the intermediary to disburse exchange funds to purchase the replacement property.

The Reverse Exchange
The IRS also allows what is known as a reverse exchange. In this case the replacement property is purchased, through the Intermediary, prior to the old property being sold. The Intermediary actually takes title to the property and holds it until the investor can find a buyer for the old property. After the replacement property is purchased, the

investor has 45 days to identify the property that will be relinquished, and 180 days from the closing of the replacement property, to close on the property being relinquished. The reverse exchange creates some financing issues since lenders don't like to lend money to the intermediary. Therefore, the investor typically needs to have the cash available to purchase the replacement property, or have a line of credit arranged.

Simultaneous Exchange
This is an exchange when the relinquished property and the replacement property closings both occur on the same day. An exchange like this is awesome if you can get two clients lined up that literally are going to exchange their property. Most exchanges are accomplished using the Delayed Exchange rules.

Delayed Exchange
This is the typical exchange where the taxpayer has 45 days after closing the relinquished property to identify the replacement property and 180 days to get it closed.

Improvement Exchange
This is an exchange where the taxpayer needs to enhance the property to create adequate value to close the exchange with creating a tax liability.

Check it out!
This was a brief overview of the 1031 Exchange concept. There are many other details with regard to a 1031 Exchange that you need to consult with your tax professional to determine what works best for you.

LEASE OPTIONS 21

The lease option tool can be a win/win situation for all parties involved. However, there are many details that need to be worked out to come to a satisfactory agreement. In Colorado, there is no Real Estate Commission approved lease option form. Therefore, licensees would be practicing law to create such an agreement for clients. With that in mind, it is always a good idea to involve an attorney to at least review the document that you intend to use on a regular basis.

The lease options I see are usually just made up of a lease that makes reference to the sales contract and then a sales contract that makes reference to the lease.

Items to negotiate within a lease option agreement:
- The rental amount per month

- Any amount of the rent that would be applied to purchase. Could be $0 or it could be the full amount of the rent. Often it is a portion, such as 20%.

- Length of Option. A year is pretty common.

- The cost of the option. The lower the amount, the less likely there will be a closing. Generally, a "buyer" wants to do a lease option because they have no money. So often times the "buyer" can't come up with an amount that will work for the seller.

- Is any part of the option refundable? Usually not. Otherwise why bother?

- Who holds the option money? Seller, Title Company, or Real Estate company.

- Is the price determined today?

- Is the price determined in the future? Sometimes based on the average of 2 appraisals at a future date.

- Does the price go up as the time in the option moves forward?

- Who pays for utilities during the lease?

- Who pays for repairs that come up during the lease, such as a broken water heater?

- Buyer Loan Qualifications. Many "buyers" want to do a lease option because they currently can't qualify for a loan. What is the likelihood they will be able to do that by the time the option expires?

FORECLOSURES AND SHORT SALES

22

When buyers come in to my office and tell me they want to purchase a foreclosure, my first question is, "what kind of foreclosure?" Most people don't realize that there are actually three phases of foreclosuure, and the process of purchasing a foreclosure can vary greatly depending on what phase their desired property is in.

FORECLOSURE PHASE 1: Short Sale

In the case of a short sale, the lender has actually not foreclosed yet. The owner is on title and usually still in possession. A short sale comes about when the amount of the loan secured by the home is in excess of current market value. The homeowner must make an application to the lender to get a short sale approved. The most important element in getting the short sale approved is the hardship letter. The owner must convince the lender, by writing a hardship letter, stating why they can no longer make payments and show they have no assets in reserve to be able to pay the loan off in full.

Depending on the market, short sales can be a nightmare for the buyers. In fact, the Colorado Real Estate Commission has a short sale addendum that gets added to the body of the purchase contract, to disclose all of the problems and issues that may come up. The biggest problem is the timing factor. In our office we have had short sale approvals that have taken up to 6 months. That might be okay if you are an investor, but it is a different story if you and your family are waiting with a full moving van and ready to move in.

FORECLOSURE PHASE 2: The bank starts foreclosure

If an owner can't sell a property with or without an approved short sale, and hasn't been making the payments, the lender will foreclose to protect their interest. After Notice of Foreclosure has been filed, the owner has some time to try to get the home sold to try to pay off the lender. If a contract is written on the home during this time frame, the Real Estate Commission has a special Foreclosure contract and addendum that we must use. Once the property is sold at the public trustee's office they no longer have any rights to the property.

FORECLOSURE PHASE 3: Bank-Ownd Property
At this point the bank has foreclosed on the property and the bank itself is now the owner of the property. This type of property is known as an REO (Real Estate Owned) or Bank Owned Property. For purchasing a property in this phase, we will use the standard Colorado purchase contract, rather than the Foreclosure contract. Most lenders will have their own addendum, prepared by their attorney, which will be added to the body of the contract.

CLIENTS WITH COLLEGE AGE CHILDREN 23

Being from a college town, I get many clients coming to me that are considering purchasing a home for their college age child to live in while attending school. You can help your clients make this a worthwhile investment financially, as well as an excellent learning experience for the student.

In Boulder, Colorado, if a parent bought a condo in the 1980s and held on to it for 4 years, they most likely would have sold it for about what they paid for it. If a parent bought a condo in the 1990s and sold it in 4 years they most likely would have made enough profit to pay for their child's education at the University of Colorado.

Owning the property the student lives in while they attend college can be beneficial in several ways.

The student will have a greater sense of stability in that they won't need to look for a different apartment to live in each year. In addition, you can pick the lifestyle that will help your student succeed in school by choosing the location and the quality of housing that best fits their needs.

In the past, apartment rents in college towns typically increase on an annual basis. By purchasing a property with a fixed rate mortgage the student's housing expense will be fixed. In addition, they won't have to deal with paying security deposits or going through the hassle of getting the deposit back.

Having a single place to live in that you own means your student will not have to worry about storing furniture over the summer break.

By purchasing a home for the student, you will be providing him/her with an excellent learning experience. The student will learn not only about the process of investing in real estate, but will also learn about the responsibilities that go along with property ownership.

In my own personal situation, I have two sons who attended the University of Colorado. I bought them each a condo using owner occupied FHA financing. Each lived in the unit and had a roommate paying rent to help pay the monthly mortgage. At the end of their college careers, they had built up some significant real estate equity to utilize in the next phase of their lives.

I have had some clients buy a piece of real estate in which they have had all two, three or more of their children live in while attending college. In some cases this spanned a 10-year time frame. Rather than throwing money down the "rent drain," they have built equity in a real estate investment over this period of time.

Helping the student establish credit

If you decide to have the student on the mortgage and deed, you can help the student establish credit prior to making a mortgage loan application by obtaining a credit card in the student's name, preferably a year prior to your purchase. In addition, if the student has a car it is a good idea to have a small loan on the car in the student's name, which can also help their credit rating.

PURCHASE WORKSHEET
To help you determine the monthly cash flow

Purchase price	$_____
Down payment	$_____
Loan amount	$_____

Monthly principal and interest payment	$_____
Mortgage insurance (if any)	$_____
Taxes	$_____
Homeowner's fee (if any)	$_____
Insurance	$_____
Net monthly expense before utilities	$_____
Total monthly cost	A $_____

Roommate rental income	$_____
Tax benefit (if any)	$_____
Total monthly income	B $_____

B - A = Net monthly profit or loss $_____

Method of Ownership for the "Student Property"

It is necessary to have your clients talk to your accountant and attorney to determine the ownership method that works best for them. Some parents will buy as a second home or as an owner occupied property with the student on the deed and loan. Others will treat it 100% as a rental property for additional tax benefits. There are many ways of holding title, including creating a Family Limited Liability Company (LLC)

Rental Roommate Income

One option is to buy a 1-bedroom condo for the student to live in by themselves. However, a 2-bedroom unit will allow for a roommate and the rent from the roommate can supplement the mortgage payment. If a 3-bedroom unit or home can be found, the rental income from 2 roommates can help the monthly cash flow even more.

Be aware that there are occupancy limits imposed in some communities. In other words, check the local ordinances before deciding if it is okay to have 5 students living in one property. In Boulder, zoning rules allow 3 unrelated people in a low-density zone and 4 unrelated people in a medium or high density zone.

Roommate Lease or Rental Agreement

Even though the potential roommates are typically close friends, it is a good idea to have a written rental agreement with roommates. The roommate rental agreement should cover all the items typically found in a residential lease such as:
- Term
- Rental rate and due date
- Security Deposit
- Notice to Vacate
- Utility payment agreement
- Maximum occupancy
- Parking
- Pets

Financing for the "Student Property"

If a condo is being purchased, the type of financing and down payment options available can be determined by the owner occupancy ratio of the condo complex, and what particular approvals (FHA, Fannie Mae, etc.) are available. It is good to have the lender check to see if the complex has the approvals for the type of financing you are considering.

Is it Better to Purchase a House or a Condo/Townhome?

This decision depends on whether or not the student will be up for doing homeownership items such as exterior maintenance, snow removal, lawn care, etc. Often a condo suits the student life the best since most college students won't be interested in mowing the lawn in their free time. Your clients will be paying a Homeowner's Association fee at a condo or townhome in order to cover these maintenance items. This will increase the monthly cost but will insure that these maintenance items are done.

Advantages of a condo for a student

- No lawn care, snow shoveling, or exterior maintenance
- Easier to "just leave" for the summer

Disadvantages of a condo for a student

- Owner occupancy ratio of the complex could affect the ability to purchase, sell, or refinance.
- Homeowner's Association fee may be high and out of your control
- Loud stereos might bother nearby neighbors

Advantages of the single family home

- No concern over occupancy ratios
- A single family home might be easier to resell than a condo since you tend to have more competing properties when selling a condo or townhome.
- Typically there is no Homeowner Association fee

Disadvantages of the single family home

- The student needs to mow & water the lawn & shovel snow
- Neighborhood may be less friendly to a group of students living there.

Disposing of your Rental Property When the Student is Ready to Move On.

When the student is ready to move on, and has hopefully graduated, there are a few options to consider. The owners can keep the property as an investment rental, the former student may keep it as their first home, or you can exchange it for a piece of investment real estate somewhere else.

As an example, I have one family I worked with, who purchased a property for their first child who attended and graduated from CU, they then sold the property in Boulder, and bought a new property in a different college town where their next child was going to attend school.

Potential financial benefits include:

- Possible appreciation in value
- Possible tax benefits
- Debt reduction on an amortized loan which increases equity build up
- Keep as an investment after college for cash flow.

RETIREMENT PLAN FUNDS- INVESTMENT IN REAL ESTATE 24

When most people think of IRAs, SEPs, 401ks, etc., they usually think of investing in the stock market or mutual funds. However, using a self-directed retirement account, your retirement plan can hold real estate, along with a variety of other real estate related investments, such as notes. Anyone can use their retirement plan to invest in real estate. You just have to have the proper plan set up. As a REALTOR®, knowing of this method of investing can potentially prove to be a great benefit for both yourself and your clients.

It has been okay to use retirement funds for investing in real estate since the 70's. It has always been the plan administrators that restricted the investment in real estate. It was never the IRS that restricted it. In fact, the idea of real estate not being allowed is so entrenched, that many CPAs are now just learning about the concept and "approving" it for their clients.

The first step is to find a plan administrator who is set up to provide self-directed plan services. Next, determine which type of retirement plan fits your situation best. The next step is to fund the account, then in turn, use those funds to purchase allowable assets.

Different Types of Retirement Investment Vehicles
Traditional IRA

- Distributions can start at 59 ½, taxable at rate at time of distribution

- Contributions are tax deductible

Roth IRA

- Distributions are TAX FREE after age 59 ½ . An advantage if an individual's tax rate is higher when distributions occur. Contributions are NOT deductible

- There are limits on the amount of income you can have to be eligible to participate in a Roth.

Simplified Employee Pension (SEP)

- For individuals who are self-employed.

Savings Incentive match Plan for Employees of Small Employers (SIMPLE)

- The SIMPLE is used by employers with 100 or fewer employees to make elective contributions for the benefit of each eligible employee.

- At 70 ½ must start taking cash or assets out of the IRA.

- Any cash or assets taken out prior to the age requirements will have a 10% penalty plus what ever the ordinary taxes on that income would be.

HSA(Health Savings Accounts) can be self directed as well.

You can even have a Roth IRA partner with your traditional IRA.

Permissible Real Estate Related Investments

You are able to invest in any form of real estate, such as single family homes, condos, multi-family, mini-storage, industrial, land, etc.

Other investments that can be done:

- **Real Estate Options.** Your plan can make a loan to another party and secure it with a note and deed of trust secured by real estate.

- **Purchase of discounted notes**

- **Share of LLC**

- **Triple Net leases**

- **You can use plan money to fund construction of improvements.** You can still invest in all other forms of "traditional" retirement account investments. In fact, you can invest in any investment allowed by law. The ability to invest in real estate in your retirement account will allow you to diversify and spread out the risk.

What You Can't Invest In (It's A Very Short List)
1. Life Insurance
2. Collectibles

Administrator of the Plan

In order to invest in real estate you must have a self-directed plan. You need to have an administrator of your plan. The administrator does not give investment advice, but only acts upon direction from you. They typically charge a fee per asset per year to administer the plan. Fees may also be structured based on the size of the account. They typically will also have a charge per check.

A company in my market place is a company called New Direction IRA, Inc., located at 1300 Plaza Ct. N #103, Lafayette, CO 80026. They can be reached at 303-546-7930. Their web site is www. NewDirectionIRA.com. The IRA holder makes all investment decisions, not the administrator.

Using Cash from your plan to buy real estate.

If your plan has a large sum of money in it you might be able to buy a property free and clear. As an example, if you had $300,000 in the plan, you could buy a single-family house. If it rented for $16,800 per year, and you had expenses for taxes, insurance, maintenance and management, after taxes, insurance, management, maintenance and misc. expenses the net cash flow might be $13,000. The net cash flow can remain in your plan and grow tax-free. You need to direct your administrator as to where to invest the cash.

Taking the next step-Buying a larger building with your plan

Then, let's say you sold the house, in the above example, for $350,000, pay no tax, and you use that as a down payment on a 12-unit apartment building. To buy the 12 unit you spend $725,000. If you use the $350,000 from the sale of the house, you will need to get a loan for $375,000. This building rents for $86,400 a year and after expenses your net cash flow is $35,000. The profit attributed to equity grows tax free but the profit because of borrowed money is taxed as UBIT. (Unrelated Business Income Tax) Explained below:

In this example the loan to value ratio was 51%, so 51% of the $35,000 would be taxed as UBIT. This example has left out transaction costs (such as commissions, loan fees etc.) for simplicity.

Using financing to buy real estate in your retirement plan

Non-recourse financing must be used for any financing required within your retirement plan. You can't be personally liable, and your plan is not a person. Non-recourse usually means that you will be required to have a larger down payment. You cannot assume recourse for your plan, but you can partner with another individual who is not a disqualified person to assume loan recourse. You must be able to make all the payments from either cash flow or Plan funds.

The typical lender that makes Fannie Mae loans will not have non-recourse financing. Non-recourse financing is available through commercial banks where an individual has a relationship or from private sources. You can partner with your IRA using your own cash. This cash can be obtained via refinancing another property you own. Locally, First Bank is making non-recourse loans for retirement plans with approximately 35% down payment. They also look at how much cash there is in the IRA to determine if the IRA can cover any negative cash flow or expenses over a period of time.

UBIT

UBIT (Unrelated Business Income Tax) is a tax on income as a result of the borrowed money rather than from the principal in the plan. In other words, if the loan is 60% of value, 60% of the income is a result of the debt financing.

Example of buying a property in your plan

Buy a $300,000 rental property in year one. Hold it for five years and lets say the value increases to $400,000. You have also averaged $500 positive cash flow a month from the property. At the end of five years you sell it for $400,000 with a $100,000 gain tax-free. You have also been accumulating cash ($500 a month x 12 x 5) to the tune of $30,000 tax-free. Obviously, the transaction is more complicated than this. You would have variable property expenses, costs of acquisition, and costs of sale, but hopefully you will get the idea. If this property were purchased outside your retirement account you would have paid tax on the gain (unless you did a 1031 exchange for another property) and tax on the cash flow at your current tax rate. If this were a ROTH IRA as you pull money out when you retire it would be tax-free.

Advantages to holding real estate in the plan

- Can buy and sell real estate at profit and pay no tax.
- Don't have to use the 1031 guidelines when trading up. There are no time restraints.
- The monthly cash flow is not taxable and grows tax free
- Can use a property manager to take care of the real estate.
- Don't have to pay taxes on the money in your plan as you save for the down payment on a piece of real estate.

Disadvantages to holding real estate in the plan

- Depreciation doesn't carry over to you personally. But the income is tax free anyway
- You can't use the property for personal use.
- Your business can't use the property.
- The plan must have the ability to cover all expenses of the property.
- For instance, real estate tax on a piece of vacant ground must be paid by the plan.
- You must be able to obtain non-recourse financing if leveraging the property.

What you can't do.

- You can't take an asset you already own and put it in the plan. The real estate must be acquired separately.
- You can't use the real estate yourself. You cannot live in it or use it for vacation purposes.
- You can't rent the property to a "disqualified" person
- You can't be compensated by your IRA, or in other words, you can't work for your IRA.
- You can't extend credit to your IRA.

Disqualified persons

1. A fiduciary of the plan
2. A person providing services to the plan
3. An employer, any of whose employees are covered by the plan.
4. An employee organization, any of whose members are covered by the plan.
5. Any direct or indirect owner of 50% or more of any of the following:
   - The combined voting power or value of all classes of stock of a corporation
   - The capital or profits interest of a partnership that is 3 or 4 above.
   - The beneficial interest of a trust or unincorporated enterprise that is #3 or #4 above.
   - A member of the family of any individual described in #1,

#2, #3, #4, or #5 above.

- Spouse
- Ancestor
- Lineal descendant
- Spouse of lineal descendant

Process for buying real estate in your plan

- Open an account with an administrator.
- Transfer or rollover funds from current plan to new one.
- Find property to purchase.
- Make offer on property. Must be in name of IRA.
- For example: New Direction IRA, FBO of Duane Duggan IRA.
- Instruct plan administrator to write earnest money check.
- If earnest money check is written personally, it should be replaced with a check from the IRA.
- Do property inspection, financing, title work, appraisal.
- Pay for any expenses using plan funds.
- Instruct plan administrator to sign closing documents and write a cashier's check for closing.
- Send deed to plan administrator.

Using an LLC (Limited Liability Company) to own the real estate

You may create an LLC to own the real estate for liability protection. The entity you create will hold the actual title to the real estate. Your retirement plan will then purchase shares in the LLC. The IRA will own the LLC. The LLC will be the signer on the contract.

Managing the Property

If you own an apartment building in your retirement plan, you can use a management company to deal with the day to day issues. Your plan administrator will actually sign the contract with the management company. The manager can collect all the rent and pay all the bills. Then the manager sends the cash flow to the plan administrator. You then direct the plan administrator where to invest the cash.

When your retirement plan sells a property

The plan administrator will sign the listing contract upon the client's direction. Once a contract is received on the property, the plan administrator will also sign the contract. The plan administrator will also sign the closing documents. The proceeds check will be made out to the retirement plan. Then the plan administrator needs to direct the cash. If you are a REALTOR®, you cannot collect a commission when selling the property out of your own plan.

UBIT also applies to the sale of the property when debt leverage financing has been used. To avoid, the IRA can pay off the loan, with IRA funds, 12 months before the property is sold.

As a REALTOR® you can do bridge loans from your IRA, but not on your own transactions or your own client's transactions.

VACATION OR SECOND HOME PURCHASE

25

As clients move along in their life, they may have purchased a personal residence or two and maybe a few investment properties. Then they start to think of getting a vacation home for their family. The REALTOR® for Life can help their clients achieve their dreams. As a vacation homeowner myself, I know the many good times and pleasures that have come about for my family as a result of that ownership.

Over the years, I have had the opportunity to refer many of my clients to REALTORS® in the spots where they want to buy a vacation home. A big part of this is knowing where my clients from Boulder like to vacation! They really like to have ski area condos at the nearby resorts and when they are tired of winter they like to go to a variety of warm island locations. I have made a special effort to know REALTORS® in those locations so I can refer them to someone that I am confident will take great care of them.

Since I own a vacation home myself, I can help my clients think through the whole process before they take that big step. There are quite a few things to consider to help them make vacation home ownership a happy experience.

- Goals for the home
- Need to rent it out to support it financially?
- If it is treated as an investment, are there any tax benefits or ramifications?
- If it's a rental, and I want to depreciate it, what are the maximum number of days it can be used?
- If it's a rental, should I manage it myself or hire a professional manager?

One of my goals for my vacation home is to leave it to my sons as a wonderful getaway and not an extra liability. We worked hard to get the property free and clear of any debt. Then I thought it would be a good idea to work on creating a legacy fund to help maintain its expenses after I'm gone.

To work toward that idea, I placed a $250,000 mortgage on the free and clear vacation home. I was lucky enough to be able to put a loan on it when interest rates were in the 3% range. I gave the $250,000 to our financial planner. The idea was to have that fund earn enough to pay the mortgage payment and still continue to grow. The mortgage is a 30-year amortization so the loan goes down each month. The goal is, 30 years from now, when I'm gone, the vacation home will be free and clear again and there will be a fund of over $300,000 to take care of it!

The idea of having a vacation home can be very exciting. However, some planning needs to be done on disposing of the property when the family is done with it, or figuring out how to keep the property in the family. If a couple has a vacation home and they have 4 kids, when the original couple dies, suddenly the property will have 4 owners. Those kids will have kids and in just 3 generations there could be 10 to 20 owners. Taking some time to create a succession plan is worth the time and effort. Generally, it is a good idea to find an attorney with experience in creating succession plans for vacation homes. They will listen to the family's wants and goals, and create a plan that works.

ALTERNATIVES TO FORECLOSURE   26

When a homeowner gets behind in their payments, they usually don't know what to do, so they do nothing. In fact, over 70% of homeowners do just that, absolutely nothing, and walk away from their homes. In reality, there are several options, with foreclosure being the last one.

A quick summary of all the different options follow:
- Reinstatement
- Repayment plan (also known as Forbearance)
- Sell the Property
- Rent the Property
- Refinance
- Modification of the Mortgage
- Short Refinance
- Deed in Lieu of Foreclosure
- Bankruptcy
- FHA and VA options
- Service members Civil Relief Act (SCRA)
- Short Sale
- Foreclosure

Reinstatement

Often, the reason the homeowner got behind on payments was only temporary. The homeowner has to pay all the missed payments, any late fees and attorney fees in a lump sum payment. After the homeowner is caught up, the loan continues as it was.

Repayment Plan or Forbearance

Sometimes the lender will take the missed payments, any late fees and attorney fees and divide them up over a payment plan or add the payments on to the end of the loan. The homeowner will usually need to show the lender why they would now be able to handle the repayment plan suggested by the lender.

Sell the Property

The more equity an owner has in their home, the more likely they will be able to sell the property and payoff the mortgage, and maybe even have something left over.

Some lenders may postpone foreclosure if they know the property is on the market or a contract is pending.

Rent the Property

The homeowner has to live somewhere. However, if the homeowner can rent a different place for less, then rent the old home, close to the total mortgage Principal, interest, taxes and insurance payment, this could be a viable alternative.

Refinance

Usually when a homeowner is behind on the payments and doesn't have a job, it is tough to get a new loan. However, if there is enough equity, the credit has not been damaged too badly, and the problem that caused the late payments has gone away, then there is a chance a new lender will make a loan.

Modification of the Mortgage

A lender may agree to a variety of modifications. Those modifications might include lowering the interest rate, extending the term of the loan, or adding the missed payments to the end of the loan.

Short Refinance

A short refinance can involve a reduction of the principal amount and possibly even a lower interest rate. Usually the borrower still needs to show not only a hardship, but also the ability to pay the mortgage at the new payment structure.

Deed-in-Lieu of Foreclosure

This usually works best when the value is about the same as the mortgage amount. It is often called the "friendly foreclosure" since the borrower simply deeds the property back to the lender. Generally, this only works if there is just one mortgage and no other liens. In the settlement, sometimes the lender will forego any rights to a deficiency judgment.

Bankruptcy

Sometimes a bankruptcy will stop a foreclosure and allow the borrower to reorganize their debt and keep their property. By entering bankruptcy, it can make the property more difficult to sell or to negotiate a short sale. Personal bankruptcy is generally considered a last resort.

FHA and VA Alternatives

If a homeowner has an FHA or VA mortgage, there might be other alternatives. More information can be found at www.fha.gov or www.homeloans.va.gov.

Service members Civil Relief Act (SCRA)

When a homeowner is called to military service, and can show that call to duty has an affect on their ability to pay, and the mortgage was placed before the active service, there can be relief.

Short Sale

A short sale occurs when the loan on the property is greater than the value of the property. When an offer comes in on the property, the lender must approve the amount of the short fall. Often times there are so many investors involved in making the decision on the short fall, it can take an extraordinary amount of time to get the final approval.

Foreclosure

Foreclosure finally comes about when the lender has filed the necessary paperwork and has served the Notice of Election and Demand. In Colorado, a sale date is then set 110 to 125 days from the NED recording date. After the sale date, there is no redemption period, and the homeowner no longer has any rights to the property.

TENANT IN COMMON INVESTMENTS (TIC)

27

As a real estate investor gets close to retirement, the thought of continuing to manage property gets more burdensome. A Tenant in Common Investment (TIC) could be just the answer. Most TICs are treated as a security, so the typical REALTOR is not licensed to sell a share in a TIC. Again, as a REALTOR for life, it is about sending your clients in the right direction. You may not earn a commission on selling a TIC because you are not licensed to, but you would likely earn a commission on selling the old building that your clients own. As I approach retirement age, I recently exchanged a 25-unit I owned, for a share of a large apartment building in Utah owned by a TIC.

Tenant In Common Investments have a few unique features:
- 35 partners maximum
- A deed is actually held by the TIC owner, so it is possible to 1031 exchange in and out. Tax and legal advice should be consulted to review the exact numbers relative to matching old debt and value with the new.
- Usually only accredited investors are allowed to invest in TICS. Again, it is necessary to work with the appropriately licensed professional to determine qualifications.
- A TIC could own apartments, shopping centers, office buildings, etc.

Advantages of a TIC
- Usually put together by many professionals with substantial resources
- No personal management
- Defer taxes if a 1031 Exchange is able to be completed
- Typically provides monthly income with a reasonable rate of return

Disadvantages
- No control over the property or risk factors
- Less liquid than a typical real estate investment

REVERSE MORTGAGES OR HOME EQUITY CONVERSION MORTGAGE (HECM)

28

In 1988 FHA reverse mortgage insurance legislation was signed by President Reagan. Though reverse mortgages have been around for some time, they are gaining popularity now as the baby boomers grow older and have high demand for cash to maintain their standard of living. If your clients are over 62 years, they could be candidates for a reverse mortgage. A reverse mortgage can even be used for the purchase of a home. The reverse mortgage process is fairly complicated and in fact, it is required for the borrower to take a class so that they have a complete understanding of the process. The REALTOR® for Life can once again send clients in the right direction on this by having a reverse mortgage professional at their fingertips. You might be helping someone stay in their home longer or you could be selling your client's large home and helping them downsize and use a reverse mortgage to buy your client's last home.

Many seniors are dependent on social security and finding it is not enough. The reverse mortgage can be a useful tool for your senior clients. This loan is designed for seniors that need to get rid of a mortgage payment and need a source of income while staying in their present home. The potential loan amount is determined using a percentage of the home's value. The percentage varies based on the age of the youngest homeowner. The homeowner still owns the home and can sell it at anytime they choose.

Typically, the homeowner will never pay off the loan. Rather, the estate of the homeowner will do that. If there is any remaining equity after death, the equity passes to the estate. If the home eventually sells for less than the balance of the reverse mortgage, the estate is not liable for that shortfall.

To get a reverse mortgage, it doesn't have to be free and clear, but there does need to be enough equity to pay off the existing mortgage and still have enough to draw upon. The loan amount available is determined by the age of the homeowners, current interest rates, and the appraised value of the home. There are several reverse mortgage calculators on the internet. However, a full time Reverse Mortgage Professional should be consulted for calculations based on current formulas.

Reverse mortgages certainly help lower income families, but the reverse mortgage has become an important part of many families' overall financial plan. Generally, the amount of equity in the home determines qualification, which is why it can be a great help to low-income seniors. In 2015, the homeowner needs to demonstrate the ability to pay taxes and insurance on the property, or set up a reserve to insure that taxes and insurance will be paid. The amount of reserve is based on a life expectancy formula.

Ideas for using a reverse mortgage
- It can provide income when the client is down to their home equity as their last source of retirement income.

- A reverse mortgage can provide income while a retirement portfolio continues to grow.

- A reverse mortgage can supplement income from an under performing retirement portfolio.

- A reverse mortgage can be used to supplement income while waiting longer to receive Social Security Benefits.

- A reverse mortgage can be used to purchase a downsized retirement home and have no payments.

Distribution of payments to the senior
The proceeds of the reverse mortgage can be distributed in lump sum, equal monthly payments, or as a line of credit with a variable interest rate. Plans may vary so it is always best to consult the provider of the reverse mortgage for individual details.

Benefits of a Reverse Mortgage
Loan proceeds are not considered income and are not taxable. May make the difference as to whether or not a senior can stay in their home by enabling the senior to get monthly income rather than make payments. The payments made to the senior are not taxable.

If there is an existing loan, it can be paid off from the initial proceeds of the reverse mortgage. The formula for the reverse mortgage prevents the mortgage from exceeding the value of the home. When the senior dies, the estate inherits the home and any equity after the reverse mortgage is paid off. There are no restrictions on what the proceeds of the reverse mortgage can be used for. A reverse mortgage is a non-recourse loan. Borrowers can never owe more than the value of the home.

Disadvantages of a reverse mortgage

The costs of getting a reverse mortgage are usually higher than getting a normal mortgage. There also could be a requirement for mortgage insurance, which adds to the upfront costs. Government assistance programs, such as Medicaid or Supplemental Security Income might be affected if too much is withdrawn in one month. The local administrator for these programs should be contacted for individual details.

Reverse mortgages are complex and the senior should get tax and legal advice if not fully understood. It is a good idea to use a loan officer that is local and specializes in Reverse Mortgages. The reverse mortgage loan is a negative amortizing loan.

What do HECM's cost?

Out of pocket costs: Generally appraisal fees and in some cases, counseling fees.

Origination Fees: This cannot exceed 2% of the first $200,000 of home value and 1% of the home value that exceeds $200,000, with a cap of $6000. An exception is that HUD allows minimum of $2500 applied to low value homes.

Initial Mortgage Insurance Premiums: this will be either .5% or 2.5% of the maximum claim amount (appraised value) depending on the amount of the available money the homeowner intends to use during the first year.

Closing Costs and Third Party Fees: Title fees, settlement fees, attorney fees, recording fees, etc.

Some of the costs may be offset by lender credits for which the homeowner may be eligible. HECM costs are generally financed into the loan so the borrower has few out-of-pocket costs.

Let's look closer at using a reverse mortgage to purchase a home (H4P) step-by-step:

1. Take the HECM counseling from a HUD counselor.
2. Determine if the applicant wishes to keep their existing home. If yes, know that the borrower will need to "income qualify" to show that there are sufficient funds to pay the existing homes

property charges as well as those of the new home.
3. If new construction: There must be a certificate of occupancy prior to beginning the process.
4. The sales contract cannot include any seller concessions and the lender may not credit any of the costs.
5. An FHA amendatory clause must be a part of the sales contract.
6. Once closed the owner must establish occupancy within 60 days.

A short example: Based on the borrower's age and expected interest rate, they may qualify for a reverse mortgage of approximately 50% of the home purchase. On a new home with a sale price of $300,000, the lender contributes 50% as the initial loan amount and the borrower brings $150,000 to closing. Only taxes, homeowners insurance and HOA fees must continue to be paid as they are due.

ESTATE PLANNING FOR REALTORS AND THEIR CLIENTS

29

If you have helped your clients build a real estate portfolio, they also need direction as to how to deal with their property in their estate. Realtors® are not licensed to give estate planning advice, but it is important for Realtors® to know when their clients need legal help. Estate planning laws are changing all the time, so in addition to getting initial advice when an estate plan is set up, it is important to have the estate plan reviewed and updated every few years. When selling a personal residence or investment property to a client, the Realtor® has the opportunity to remind their clients to get an estate plan update. This advice is especially important as clients move in from out of state. Even if your client has an estate plan, many plans won't work because they haven't been updated to keep in tune with current laws.

Over my career, when I have asked clients if they have a will and an estate plan, I have been surprised at the huge number of people that just want to avoid the process. However, a little effort in planning saves money and headaches when the inevitable happens.

Proper planning can help your clients avoid probate. If your clients own real estate and die without a will and an estate plan, the will is settled through the process of probate. The probate process does not always transfer property in the way the deceased really might have wanted it to go.

The goal of estate planning

Most people would like to be able to control their real estate while they are alive, but also want to plan for what happens if they become disabled or die prematurely. They want to give what they have to whom they want, when they want, and in the way they want.

How to hold title

Realtors® often find themselves being asked how to hold title to real estate. First of all, the REALTOR® should not be giving advice on how to hold title. However, they do need to know a few basics.

The most common mistake is when a married couple with children from a prior marriage decide to hold title to their home in joint tenants. If their wish is to let their children from the first marriage inherit interest in real estate, rather than the new spouse, joint tenants is the wrong answer. Tenants in Common will more likely direct ownership in the way that they intend.

Being from a college town, parents often buy real estate for their children to live in while they attend college. A joint tenant is not automatically the best answer here either. Often, when clients meet with an estate-planning attorney, it is suggested they own the property in a living trust. This is usually determined by the overall size of the estate.

Investment Property
As a client's portfolio grows, it is important to review whether real estate should be held by an LLC or some other entity. Tax and legal counsel should always be consulted as clients make these decisions.

Advantages of holding property in an LLC
- Creates a legal shield
- Can sell off shares of the LLC
- The property owned by the LLC functions more like a real business

Disadvantages of holding property in an LLC
- Costs of creating the LLC
- Separate tax return needs to be filed each year for the entity

CHARITABLE INVESTMENT TRUSTS 30

As a person nears the end of their life, they might start to feel charitable, even if they never have before! A Charitable Remainder Trust could be something to set up to provide income while still alive, and a nice gift to their favorite charity after death. Again, REALTORS® don't set these up, so tax and legal advice is needed to determine if this is something that works for anyone's given situation.

What is a Charitable Remainder Trust?

A Charitable Remainder Trust is a special tax-exempt irrevocable trust arrangement written to comply with federal tax laws and regulations. You transfer cash or assets (especially appreciated assets) to the trust and may receive income for life or, if you choose, a certain term of years (not to exceed 20). In fact, the income can be paid over your life, your spouse's life, and even your children's and grandchildren's lives.

What section of the IRS code governs whether a trust qualifies as a CRT?

IRS code section 664 lists the requirements a trust must meet in order to qualify as a Charitable Remainder Trust. The Charitable Remainder Trust was made possible by the Tax Reform Act of 1969.

OWNER FINANCING   **31**

When a seller has a considerable amount of equity in a home, they might consider financing the purchase for a buyer. Owner financing might be an attractive investment opportunity depending on what other investments are competing for those dollars at the time.

In the past, it was fairly simple for an owner to finance. In Colorado, for example, we had standard notes and deeds of trusts that licensed real estate agents were able to fill out based on the terms negotiated in a state approved contract. The onset of Dodd-Frank and the Consumer Financial Protection Bureau (CFPB), which took effect January 10, 2014, created many new rules and regulations with which sellers of residential 1–4 units must comply. In order for a seller to comply, they should seek assistance from a licensed attorney or Mortgage Loan Officer (MLO).

Possible advantages for a seller to do owner financing:

- Higher rate of return compared to many other investment alternatives.

- Secured with a deed of trust, or similar document, with real estate familiar to the seller in the event of a default.

- Regular monthly income.

Possible disadvantages for a seller to do owner financing:

- Ties up the money until loan is paid off.
- Might have to go through the foreclosure process in the event of default.

In general, Dodd-Frank says that if a loan will be secured by a property that the borrower will live in, the person who places the loan with the borrower must be a MLO. However, there are exclusions that allow sellers to finance without being an MLO, if they meet certain qualifications.

Exclusions:
Three property exclusions:

- Sellers can only finance three or fewer 1 – 4 unit residential properties in a 12 month period.
- The properties must have been owned by the seller.
- The properties must be the security for the loans.
- Seller cannot be a builder in the normal course of their business.
- The loan must be fully amortizing.
- Seller must reasonably determine the consumer's ability to repay.
- The loan must have a fixed interest rate or have an adjustable rate that is fixed for at least five years.
- If the rate is adjustable, it must be indexed with a widely available index such as LIBOR.

One property exclusions:

- When a seller is only financing a single 1-4 unit residential property in a 12 month period.
- The seller can only be an individual, estate or trust. Corporations, LLC's, etc. don't qualify.
- Seller cannot be a builder in the normal course of their business.
- The loan cannot have negative amortization.
- Balloon payments are permissible. The loan does not have to be fully amortized.
- The loan must have a fixed interest rate or have an adjustable rate that is fixed for at least five years.
- If the rate is adjustable, it must be indexed with a widely available index such as LIBOR.

The above rules are from Dodd-Frank at the federal level. Any seller offering owner financing needs to check with a local attorney or MLO to determine if there are any state requirements that need to be met for compliance. Failure of the seller to comply with Dodd-Frank and any state requirements could have an effect on the ability to enforce foreclosure if the borrower were to default.

DUANE'S TOP TEN TIPS FOR REALTOR® FOR LIFE SUCCESS

32

It is early in the year. Have you done your plan for the year or are you already working your plan? If you aren't already working your plan, then you are already behind for the year. In fact, success in real estate is really a month to month lease. You have to keep moving ahead to stay competitive in the business. Over the years you could have subscribed to Tommy Hopkins, the Howard Brinton Star Power tapes, been a Mike Ferryite, a Rick Deluca dude and many more. All these have been excellent sources of information to help keep REALTORS® at the top of their game. But through it all, and whether you have been in the business 1 year or 25 years, the basic elements of success in our industry are the same. So here are my Top 10 Tips for you to kick off an incredible year, each and every year. Sorry if there are a few clichés included here, but some things have just stuck in my mind!

1. Plan your work, work your plan.

If you don't know where you are going, how will you know when you get there? Plus, you'll never do better than you plan to. Your plan should include how you intend to help your clients receive the best possible real estate service from you. REALTORS® who provide the best service, in their client's eyes, will naturally be rewarded the best.

Your planning should include a business plan and a marketing plan. If you have never done a business plan, get some help to do it right the first time. Lay out how you are going to get business. It can be fun to plan out your year. In fact, it can be so much fun that all that ever happens is planning. Don't forget to TAKE ACTION! Don't just talk the talk. Be sure to walk the walk.

Set Business Goals. You should have a business goal that sets out a quantity of business. This quantity can be number of closings, number of families helped, commission dollars, or whatever unit of measurement you choose to use. Whatever the unit of measurement, it is the level of business you need to reach to achieve your dreams. To help you monitor your progress it is a good idea to have a weekly, monthly, annual and even a 5-year goal. Remember, a goal is not a goal without a date on it.

Learn delayed gratification. Reap what you sow. Real estate is not a salaried business. You have to plant the seeds of success many months ahead of the harvest.

Your Dream or Your "Why." In order to keep going every day you need to have a dream or a "why." It is much easier to keep plugging away at your goal when you have a purpose. That dream could be a vacation, a new house, or a fully funded college education for your child. Whatever it is, make it yours and keep it in focus!

2. Show up and be on time.

Execute your plan by showing up and treating your real estate business like a job! In real estate you work for yourself. There is no one checking to see if you arrive at the office at 8:00 am. If you were your "boss", would you be impressed with your own work ethic? If you show up at work and are on time with your clients, you have taken one step in the right direction.

Schedule personal time just like business time and stick to it. Make a schedule of an ideal day for you. Include the activities that are the most productive for you (like showing property) and also the necessary activities (like picking the kids up from school).

Treat your real estate career like a business. Consider becoming your own corporation. You can visit with your CPA on the advantages and disadvantages. One thing becoming a corporation does is it makes you treat your business like a business rather than running it out of a shoebox. You have to pay yourself at regular intervals. (Wow, quite a concept in real estate!) You have to do regular tax withholdings on each paycheck and the list goes on and on. When you have a real business, whether it's a corporation, or just a tight ship, your clients will notice!

3. Be Prepared

It has often been said that if you show up, are on time and are prepared, you have done 80% of what it takes to be successful. With the internet, your clients now have more market information than they did in the past. You need to be more prepared than your client and take the service you provide to the next level.

Your clients are looking for you to "add value" to their knowledge and experience, just like what you look for in a new computer. Remember what we used to pay for a computer with 1/3 the power at twice the price? Today consumers are looking at more value from us, at less expense. Will you step up and deliver? How do you do that? By being prepared and offering more than you did in the past.

4. Just Call 'em

Number four is the world's shortest real estate success seminar. To be successful you have to talk to people. If you are wondering if a buyer prospect might be interested in a new listing, don't wonder too long...just call 'em! Once you have established a business relationship with someone the "No Call" rules no longer come into play. Once you get permission to call someone, don't hesitate...just call 'em! If you prefer your prospecting in person, remember the "see twenty people belly to belly each day" rule.

5. Technology, the Internet, and Change

Harness it and use it to your advantage. Technology can make your job easier, but it doesn't replace the people part of our business. Use technology to get your job done more quickly, accurately, and more efficiently for your clients than ever before. Technology has changed how we do everything. Our human nature is to resist change and keep things "the way they are." But, the REALTOR® who grasps technology will be able to move ahead at the same pace as their clients. Since the average REALTOR® is over 40 years old, many are having a tough time making technology adjustments. Learn the new technology and don't make uninformed decisions on new technology based on how old technology performed in the past.

Buyer and Seller Prospecting on the internet has forever changed our marketing. Study the many different options on the internet to figure out what works best for you.

6. Get involved!

The successful REALTOR® is the involved REALTOR®. Get involved with your REALTOR® Association. By being involved you learn what is going on in our industry today and you can literally help shape the future of our industry and your business.

Wear your REALTOR® "R" with pride! The National Association of REALTORS® has had a study performed that says the value of the REALTOR® trademark is worth $32,000 to the average REALTOR® over a 10-year period.

Get involved with life! If you are active in your community, whether it is church, your kid's soccer team or knitting club, you'll be a better citizen and a better REALTOR®.

Get involved with your company. If you are with a national franchise, get involved at the national level and build your own referral network. If you aren't in a national franchise you can still get involved at the national and international level through our REALTOR® organization.

7. Education

It's not brain surgery. Lets face it, to get started in your real estate career you don't have to pursue the same educational route that a brain surgeon does. Yet, the public is trusting the REALTOR® to help them with what is typically the biggest financial decision of their life. You owe it to yourself and your clients to continue your education so you can provide the best possible service.

Education can come in a wide variety of forms. Your clients expect you to know the market. You educate yourself by being "in" the market, by previewing homes, showing homes, doing market evaluations, etc.   In addition to practicing real estate, you can educate yourself by earning professional REALTOR® designations or following the recommendations of a Business Coach. Our Colorado and National Association of REALTORS® also provide excellent educational opportunities at their respective annual conventions.

In today's world, you don't even need to go anywhere to educate yourself! You can read books and listen to digital voice on your MP3 player or IPOD®. You can use the NAR website to stay informed on current issues.

8. Stay in one place.

Many years ago the National Association of REALTORS® did a study to determine the most common ingredients to success. One of those ingredients was being in one place for 5 years. Your clients need to know where you are to find you! Office hoppers, blaming the company for their woes, tend to be the least successful.

9. Attitude

The amount of business you have is all about your attitude! In fact, when the market is "slower" there are more opportunities to get paid because your clients need you more!

Have you heard about "The Man Who Sold Hot Dogs"? Maybe you can relate this story to your real estate business. There once was a man who sold hot dogs on the streets of Manhattan. He had a son who he hoped to send to college. The man worked hard almost stopping people in the street to sell his hot dogs. He took care in getting the best ingredients he could afford and prepared them to his utmost ability. In the mornings before lunch, he would take flyers around to the places people worked that advertised his hot dog stand as a great place for lunch. The man maintained a booming hot dog business.

When his son was old enough to go to college, he had saved enough money to send him by selling hot dogs. His son was educated in a fine business school. His son learned about business cycles, economics, and recessions. When his son returned from college and he saw his Dad in the booming hot dog business, he said "Haven't you heard Dad? We're in a recession and business is slow. Why are you working so hard?" Now, having never been to college, the man who sold hot dogs reasoned, "Well, my son has been to college and he says business is slow". The man that sold hot dogs figured business was bad, so he didn't try to stop people on the street to buy his hot dogs any more. He stopped dropping flyers off at the places people worked. Business started to drop off, so he had to start cutting back on the quality of ingredients. People didn't like the taste of his hot dogs anymore and stopped coming. Soon, no one was buying his hot dogs any more at all. He said, " You know, my college educated son is right. Business IS bad".

Whether you are a new REALTOR® or a veteran, act like its impossible to fail, regardless of "the market". Be excited before going into a listing presentation or meeting with a buyer for the first time. Show that you are the best and believe in what you do.

Have an attitude of belief! You need a belief in real estate as a profession and in your company as well as belief in yourself and your abilities. Have an attitude of commitment. You need to be able to say to yourself you're going to do what ever it takes to build your business. If you are having trouble making a commitment, you are still negotiating the price of success.

10. Invest in real estate
Invest in what you sell. Can you imagine a stockbroker who doesn't own any stock? How about a REALTOR® that doesn't own a home or

investment property? Set an example for your clients and invest in real estate as soon as you can. Now is a good time.

Invest for retirement. Not only should you invest in real estate, you should learn how to invest in real estate using your retirement funds. Once you know how yourself, teach your clients.

ACKNOWLEDGMENTS

I want to thank the following experts in their field for their professional guidance in creating this book.

Trevor Bellows, *Premier Mortgage*

Rick Burger, *Property Manager*

Robert Groening, *Reverse Mortgages*

Karl Frank, *A and I Financial Services, TICs (Tenant in Common Investments)*

William Humphrey, *IRA investing*

Donald Kaniecki, *Tax Issues*

ABOUT THE AUTHOR

Duane Duggan is a third generation native of Colorado and a graduate of the University of Colorado Business School with a major in real estate. Currently, Duane and his Team, The Boulder Property Network at RE/MAX of Boulder, have been consistent top producers in Boulder County residential and investment real estate sales since 1978! Duane has been a RE/MAX agent since 1982, has been a regular member of the RE/MAX Chairman's Club and has been awarded the RE/MAX International Lifetime Achievement Award and the Circle of Legends Award. Duane has facilitated over 2,500 transactions over his career and the fact that the vast majority of his business comes from repeat and referred clients, provides further testimony to the high level of Service and Expertise provided by Duane and his team!

Duane is a firm believer in giving back to his Community and Profession and has done so by contributing his Time and Expertise to numerous local Non-Profit Organizations and by being a mentor and business coach to other REALTORS. Duane is actively involved in the local and state Boards of REALTORS. He served as the President of the Boulder Area REALTOR Association in 2005 and has held various positions with the Colorado Association of REALTORS, including North East District Vice President and Colorado State Spokesperson.

Made in the USA
Columbia, SC
13 June 2019